Coming Home to Yourself

Eighteen Wise Women Reflect on Their Journeys

Patricia Gottlieb Shapiro, MSW

Coming Home to Yourself

Eighteen Wise Women Reflect on Their Journeys

Gaon Books

Gaon Books
P.O. Box 23924
Santa Fe, NM 87502

www.gaonbooks.com

Library of Congress Cataloging-in-Publication Data

Shapiro, Patricia Gottlieb.
Coming home to yourself: eighteen wise women reflect on their journeys /
Patricia Gottlieb Shapiro.
p. cm.
Includes bibliographical references.
ISBN 978-1-935604-02-0 (alk. paper)
1. Older women. 2. Older women--Anecdotes. 3. Social change. 4. Social evolution. I. Title.
HQ1061.S4527 2010
305.26'2--dc22

2010028014

Manufactured in the United States of America.
The paper used in this publication is acid free and meets all ANSI (American National Standard for Information Sciences) standards for archival quality paper.

British Cataloguing-in-Publication data for this book is available from the British Library.

Cover Design by Gloria Abella Ballen

Also by Patricia Gottlieb Shapiro

Yoga For Women At Midlife & Beyond: A Home Companion

Heart To Heart: Deepening Women's Friendships At Midlife

My Turn: Women's Search For Self After The Children Leave

Always My Child: A Parent's Guide To Understanding Your Gay, Lesbian, Bisexual, Transgendered Or Questioning Son Or Daughter (with coauthor)

A Parent's Guide To Childhood And Adolescent Depression

Women, Mentors & Success (with coauthor)

Caring For The Mentally Ill

"We may act sophisticated and worldly but I believe we feel safest when we go inside ourselves and find home, a place where we belong and maybe the only place we really do."

Maya Angelou, *Letter to My Daughter*

For Sierra and Maelle

Contents

Acknowledgments

In some ways, a book about eighteen women is like an iceberg. Beneath the women whose stories you'll read lies a whole network of other women—and a few good men—who have helped make this book a reality.

So many people were helpful in suggesting participants for the book and in introducing them to me. Tanya Taylor Rubinstein was most generous with her many leads. She connected me to Candace Walsh, who led me to a reporters' referral service called HARO (Help a Reporter Out), which resulted in many eager queries and in three sterling leads whose stories you'll read in this book. For other referrals, I want to thank Marilyn Batts, Vee Bybee, Dick Goldberg, Lorraine Schechter, Marian Sandmaier, Elaine Pinkerton and Ron Duncan Hart.

My gratitude goes out to the women profiled in this book. They are an extraordinary group of women who have overcome personal challenges to continue growing and seeking until they reached their own internal home. They were giving of their time, their emotions and their experiences with me.

I'm also appreciative of the bigheartedness of the women who queried me about being a part of this book but were not included for various reasons. I was impressed by their ability to share so openly and freely before they even knew me and to take the time to write long emails about their lives, knowing they might not be a part of the book.

For their careful reading of the manuscript and for their insightful, sensitive comments, I want to thank Martha Jablow, who read every word in this book and Lorraine Schechter, who read almost every word. My thanks also goes to Anne Angerman, Margo Bachman, Gabrilla Hoeglund and Dick Shapiro, who read select chapters.

It has been a pleasure to work with my publisher, Ron Duncan Hart. He has been enthusiastic about this project from the beginning and steady and caring in his commitment to this book and to me.

As I complete this manuscript, I've just started to think about marketing the book. While this list is incomplete, I am grateful to my sister Anne Angerman, to Susan Berk, and to Dick Goldberg for their networking and support.

My friends, in Santa Fe and Philadelphia, have been there for me during this long, creative process, as always. I could not have written this book without their continued encouragement and caring. A special thank you goes to Lorraine Schechter, who has shared her wisdom on many aspects of this project during our long walks and conversations.

I am grateful to my husband Dick for his continued confidence in me, his encouragement and his loving presence in my life. To my immediate family—my daughter and son-in-law Margo and Nicolai Bachman and my son and daughter-in-law Andrew and Corrie Shapiro—I want to express my love and appreciation for their unwavering support and affection.

Lastly, I've dedicated this book to my two granddaughters, Sierra Bachman and Maelle Shapiro, who are too young to read. I thought of them often while I was writing this book, wondering whether they would find their path to their deepest selves as young women or would grapple with these issues into their later years like their grandmother's generation. My hope is that they will always be true to themselves and follow their inner compass, rather than looking for approval and acceptance in the external world and in other people. When they are old enough to understand this book, I hope it will guide them on their journey home.

Introduction

"All language is a longing for home," wrote Rumi, the thirteenth century poet. In the twenty-first century, I'd take that a step further and say that the longing for home *itself* is a powerful force, especially as we get older.

And what is that home we hunger for? Home means many things to different people. It can be a physical place, an emotional space, or an activity where we can be ourselves, where we can reveal our true nature and be known for who we are. It is a source of inner peace and inspiration, both a journey and a destination.

Oprah Winfrey described this sense of coming home in the September 2008 issue of *O Magazine* when she wrote about how she remedied her feeling of being overwhelmed in the aftermath of the crisis at the school she developed in South Africa the previous year:

"I pulled out my gratitude journal, in which I'd been too tired to write even a sentence for months. I went to my favorite place on earth, the place where 12 oaks form a canopy.... I watched the sunlight filter between the branches and enhance every leaf. I listened to the birds....

"I let myself absorb the sacredness and dignity of the oaks. I let those trees remind me how to be: still. I took a few deep breaths. I said 'Thank you' out loud. I felt like I'd come home."

In Oprah's case, a physical place transported her "home" to her true self. Other women come home when they stand in front of an easel painting, play Mozart on their violin, or meditate. As you meet the eighteen women in this book who each followed a different path home, you'll see that home is both the activity and the feeling it engenders. Home is that feeling of wholeness, which is with us no matter where we are or whom we're with. We take it with us wherever we go, because it resides within our own head and heart.

Growing up with a family in the furniture business, I've always been interested in the concept of home. My physical home was a red brick house at 432 Wolf Street in a working class neighborhood two blocks from Lake Michigan in Racine, Wisconsin. Our home was the center for every holiday dinner since none of my extended family cooked. My mother would roast the brisket and potatoes, boil the vegetables, bake the sour cream coffee cake, and brew the coffee for every Thanksgiving and Passover and each minor holiday in between. All the cousins gathered at our house, sitting around the huge open fireplace. I felt so happy with everyone there.

It took me years to recreate that same feeling when I was living in Philadelphia with a family of my own, and my parents, relatives and sister were hundreds of miles away. Since our family was small, I invited friends to join us, so our holidays became a fusion of family and friends, and I developed a reputation for making friends feel like family. Today, living in Santa Fe, nothing makes me happier than having all my children and grandchildren under one roof, and if friends need a place to celebrate the holidays, of course, they are welcome too.

Growing up, I was an only child for four years and then my sister and I were one of the few children in a family top heavy with adults. As the first child, I felt pressure to obey the rules and be good, or as my sister Anne would say, "Patti was always perfect" (in her eyes).

Of course, I wasn't perfect, but I tried to please my parents and win their approval by conforming to their wishes. One incident stands out: I remember sitting in the back seat of the Pontiac with my parents up front. I was sixteen years old, and we were going to pick up my cousin Lillian for her brother Ted's funeral. Ted, one of my favorite older cousins, had dropped dead from a heart attack in his fifties while fishing in the Canadian wilderness. I was sitting in the back seat quietly crying when Mother turned around and said sharply, "Stop crying. Don't let anyone see you cry! You'll upset Lillian."

Because of occurrences like this, I learned to hide my feelings under a placid veneer and not reveal my emotions. I became so adept at this that after awhile, I didn't know how I felt. It wasn't until I went to social work school and had to acknowledge and report every feeling—on waking, in the shower, throughout the day—that I started getting back in touch with my feelings.

I wrote my master's thesis on the use of spontaneity in the casework situation. That was the beginning of my interest in being authentic, a theme that has been consistent throughout my writing.

Because I was unable to find part-time social work when my children were small, I turned to writing, something I had always longed to do. I wrote on topics that interested me professionally: personality profiles and feature articles on health, medicine, and psychological issues. With my social work background as a foundation, I was comfortable writing about people and their problems. After writing research-based nonfiction for ten or twelve years, I yearned for something more, something deeper. As I approached my fiftieth birthday, I felt a need to write from my heart.

That's when I started writing about my own personal experiences. I wrote about my challenges after my children left home, my friendships at midlife, my relationship with my sister, and what yoga meant to me. I still had to do research, but now I enriched the research with my own narrative. Since I am a private person, this proved difficult at first, but as I shared more I was able to unearth my own voice, reveal my impressions and emotions, and connect more intimately with others.

As I moved further away from the intellectual, I was ripe for an experience "beyond the mind." In my early fifties, I was going through a difficult time and needed something to help me cope. I decided to try yoga. I loved it from the moment I walked into my first class in a studio bathed in white. Even before I started moving and breathing consciously, I felt a huge sense of relief. I had walked in uptight and edgy, not having slept the night before. When I walked out after that first class, I was in a very different place. I knew the problems were still there but somehow they seemed more distant, and I was able to handle them better. From the nurturing I received and the connection I felt, I couldn't wait to go back for more. There was no question that yoga would be an important piece of my life from then on.

Since that first class eighteen years ago, yoga has been my daily companion. In my last book, *Yoga For Women At Midlife & Beyond: A Home Companion,* I wrote: "Yoga is a homecoming: a coming home to ourselves." And that's exactly how I feel—every single day.

More recently, yoga helped me return to my other "home": writing. After completing my last book in 2005, I didn't think I'd write another one. With no inspiration, my ideas had dried up, and I felt that my life as a writer was over. Nonetheless, I continued to call myself a writer—even though I wasn't writing. During this period, I knew something was missing. I felt unsettled and unproductive, but couldn't quite figure out what was going on. I took poetry classes, dabbled in book arts and sampled the rich cultural scene in Santa Fe. Although these activities were enjoyable, they didn't satisfy me on a visceral level as my writing had.

The one thing that grounded me during this disconcerting period was my yoga practice. Through doing meditation, yoga and breath work, I was able to connect to who I truly am, reflect on what I wanted to do with my life, and gain clarity about what mattered most to me.

Then I spent a week devoted to authors at The Chautauqua Institution in a beautiful wooded location on a clear lake in upstate New York. Each day different authors spoke about their work, about the writer's life, and about their own journey as an author. There were poetry readings, talks on memoir writing, and book signings. I felt drawn to writing and writers as never before and journaled with a fervor in that rich, nourishing atmosphere. I left that week knowing that I wanted to write again and be a part of the creative fabric of Santa Fe. The idea for this book began to percolate and emerge as I threw myself into journal writing on my return, reflected on the meaning of home as we age, and discussed these ideas with friends.

Yoga is my home. It doesn't matter whether I'm standing on one foot in tree pose on my mat in my own bedroom or in a motel room a thousand miles away: I feel centered and grounded. When I come off the mat, I take that feeling with me and it gives me comfort and confidence to be myself—wherever I am or whoever I'm with.

Knowing this about myself, I wondered what path others would take or what they needed to do to reach the same sense of wholeness that I receive from yoga. I imagined that there were many ways to come home but was curious about whether the process was universal for older women with only the content and context different.

Did it matter what their cultural and religious background was or what part of the country they lived in? Was it significant whether they were straight or gay, rich or poor? Would they all arrive at the same destination at the end of their journey? And, most importantly, how would they know when they'd arrived?

Searching for answers to these questions motivated me to find a diverse, multi-cultural group of women to include in my book. I sent out a "Call for Stories" on the Internet to friends, acquaintances and colleagues and received a torrent of replies; many women wrote to me wanting to be a part of this book. It was not unusual to receive two to three paged single-spaced replies in which women poured out their life stories. They'd often end with a comment like, "If this is not what you want, don't worry. Getting information about your project was the inspiration I needed to take the time to reflect on these experiences and put them into words." Truly an amazing response!

Many sent information about a career change they'd made, but this book is not about career change. It is about something much deeper and more fundamental: It is about experiencing a turning point later in life that transforms our self-concept and our self-perception as we learn about ourselves and the world, and look at ourselves differently through the lens and wisdom of our sixty-plus years.

Through an elaborate screening process, I was able to winnow down the applicants and select eighteen women. I have chosen the number eighteen, because it is a spiritual number in Judaism. The Hebrew word for "alive" or "life" is *chai*, which has a numerical value of eighteen. Jews often give donations and monetary gifts in multiples of eighteen as a way to convey blessings for a long life. I'm using it in my title as a symbolic way to honor the richness of the lives and the longevity of the women featured in the book.

These women are truly remarkable. They are courageous, outspoken, feisty and determined. In working with me, they were generous with their time and open in sharing their life stories. They are not celebrities but women like you and me.

I did not include women who had found their path years ago and followed it through midlife into their sixties and seventies, like my friends Lorraine and Diane, who knew from a young age, with a single-minded focus, that they would be artists and that art was their passion and their home. I was fascinated by women who followed an established path or lived a life without intention for years and then experienced this turning point or an insight or revelation that transformed their sense of self and changed their lives in profound ways. Victoria Zackheim, a writer and editor whom you'll get to know in this book, would have told you that life was good two years ago. Her work was satisfying, the anthologies she edited received rave reviews, and her twin granddaughters brought her much joy. But everything changed in the summer of 2008: she fell down the stairs of her loft. Actually, her life *outwardly* did not change that much, but the internal shifts from the fall dramatically altered her life. As you'll read in her chapter, she discovered her fragility, came to terms with her mortality, and developed a newfound ability to accept help from friends and family.

Like Victoria, each woman I've written about has her own chapter, which consists of two parts: It begins with her profile, summing up her life to the present; this is followed by a larger section in which she speaks in her own words, which I've developed from our interviews, about how she found her "home," her path of getting there, and how this process transformed her view of herself and her world.

I am hoping that the women in this book, who range in age from fifty-six to seventy-seven, will serve as role models and inspiration for younger women who are interested in actualizing themselves. While someone who is forty or fifty may think she can't identify with a woman who is sixty or seventy, once she reads these stories, I know she'll feel a strong connection to these extraordinary women and abandon the common stereotypes that older women are invisible, dull, and "over the hill."

Home is a haven within where we can express ourselves without masks or airs, where we can be authentic and feel comfortable and safe. It is different from finding a resting place in troubled times; it is an emotional and psychological state that creates the sense of belonging and well-being we crave. It is a sense of harmony: our internal and external selves matching, our inner and outer voices becoming one. Home is an emotional experience that grounds us and gives us a sense of contentment. At earlier periods in our lives we may have felt we were inadequate, but not anymore. At forty when her ex-husband was leaving, Elena Montano, whom you'll meet on these pages, says, "I felt ugly, old and terrible. Today at seventy, I feel younger, I love myself, and I take good care of me." Thirty years made a huge difference in her self-concept.

At this stage, we know we're not perfect and certainly not finished growing, but we're in a very different space than when we were younger. We are not constantly second guessing ourselves or desperately seeking approval of everyone we meet. If "they" don't like us, that's their problem. After participating in a panel discussion, a friend told me, "It took me sixty-five years to find my voice. When I spoke, I felt grounded and solid, and I didn't care if I offended anyone."

We laugh that sixty is the new forty, and there's actually some truth to it. Sixty is no longer old, but it's also very different from fifty. Like the fifties, the sixties and seventies can be full of vitality and life, but with a twist: there's a recognition of how fleeting time is and how precious each moment is. As you'll see when you meet the women in this book, they are seeking new pursuits, following their dreams, exploring their creativity in original ways. They are not content to rest on their laurels—or in their rocking chairs on the front porch! Their age does not stop them or deter them from continuing to grow and develop. Many have said, in fact, that this is the best time in their lives, that they've never been more content, and that their days are richer and fuller than in the past. They are looking forward to the years ahead with optimism.

Of course, you can come home to yourself at any age, but something different happens when we grow older. We have a seasoned perspective that we don't have when we're younger. We have a long history and by now, we know what's important and what's not. After our children leave home, we can focus on ourselves (often for the first time) and seek out our passions as a way to fulfill ourselves now that our active mothering role is over. At times, there is a frenetic searching for something—anything—to fill the void. By the time we reach our sixties, we've settled on "something"—be it opening a small consulting business, feeding the homeless, or teaching tai chi. Our wide-ranging search over, we are able to delve deeper now.

For women who have not had children, midlife and the years beyond offer an opportunity to reflect on the past and fulfill those dreams that have been on the back burner for years.

Whether they've had children or not, women who have passed their sixtieth birthday often struggle with the question: How can I live my life in a meaningful way? Recognizing the limited time left motivates us to spend the remaining years wisely and consciously, taking into consideration the physical limitations and challenges that occur as we age.

We must contend with emotional issues as well: coming to terms with regrets, facing concerns and anxieties about getting older, and losing friends and family members. We come to realize that our past is longer than our future and we'd better seize the moment now or we'll lose it. *Now* is the time to take that extra weekend at the beach, pay another visit to a grandbaby, or ride in a hot air balloon.

As we get older, we often yearn to reconnect with childhood or college friends. One of my friends went to a spa with five high school buddies to celebrate their fiftieth birthday. Another began an annual retreat several years ago with six college friends, most of whom she hadn't spoken to in thirty years. Bonding with these friends later in life gives us a deeper sense of who we truly are—and who we could still be—and can be an important piece in retrieving our younger selves for the process of coming home.

Not everyone, however, has come home to their true selves by the time they reach sixty years of age. "I've spent years searching for my home," a friend told me over tea recently, "and at sixty-four, I still haven't found it." Like many women, she continues her search, knowing that she must find her own sense of contentment and peacefulness to complete herself before she dies.

Initially, I thought I'd explore home in four distinct ways: as a physical place, like the ocean, mountains or a room of one's own; as a spiritual practice, such as meditation or a religious belief; as a passion, like painting, writing or acting; and as a connection to someone special, such as a partner, friend or grandchild. But life is messy. No one is able to compartmentalize her life in this way. As I interviewed woman after woman, I had to abandon these distinctions and listen for the unspoken connections as women shared their rich, multi-faceted lives with me.

I was also listening for answers to those questions that spurned this project. The main question focused on how culture, religion, lifestyle, geographic location, or economics made a difference in the homecoming process. A secondary interest was the frequency of a focused spiritual path on the journey home. As you read this book, you'll learn that *all* these women yearned to come home to their deepest selves. Their paths were varied and distinctive; some had tremendous support while others forged on alone. Some took much longer while others had a more direct path. But no matter what their starting point, how long or circuitous their path, or how much support they had, all the women arrived at the same internal destination.

They all came to a place within themselves of comfort and familiarity, of harmony and wholeness, of accepting and loving themselves. In other words, they became authentic. They dropped their social mask, stopped searching in the external world for approval and acceptance, and learned that what they had been seeking all along was within themselves. They simply had to acknowledge it, accept it, and then celebrate it.

This is not to say that any of us is "done." As long as we're alive, there will be stumbling blocks and hurdles to overcome, but arriving home gives us the foundation and strength to meet these challenges with confidence. Christine Johnson expressed this sentiment well in her chapter. She told me, "I'm never home and *settled*. I may be home, in a spot where I'm comfortable for three, six months, even a year, and then I realize that something else needs to be done with me as a person so I can be a better mother, a better grandmother, a better Christian, a better friend. I don't see it as, 'Well, I'm here now. I've arrived.' There's always room for growth."

For you, the reader, I hope the women in this book will inspire you to find your way home to your deepest self. If you've already had this experience, then you will enjoy reading about other women's journeys. If you're still searching, these women's stories can motivate you to continue your quest. Wherever you are in the process, be assured that you are not alone. Generations of women support you on your journey and welcome you to find your own authentic home.

Edie Elkan

Recapturing a Lost Dream

Edie Elkan is a believer in dreams: lost dreams, found dreams, and impossible dreams. Her life is an example of never giving up and holding on to a dream for years, whether it's about finding your father or recapturing something in your life that feels incomplete.

Edie's philosophy is not surprising considering that her mother's family left Odessa, Russia to follow a dream of their own of a better life. They settled in Philadelphia in 1910 and joined a community of Russian Jews there; her mother didn't speak English until she went to kindergarten. Imagine the shock and horror when, years later, she came home with a dashing Midwestern Catholic man in uniform. Of course, she wouldn't listen to her parents' protestations: she was head-over-heels in love with him. They married after dating for only seven weeks and took off for California where his family lived.

A flight engineer, he was sent overseas during World War II and on one of his trips home, Edie was conceived; her father was still abroad when she was born in 1945. He returned when she was nine months old and they all piled into their black Hudson and took Route 66 across the country to Philadelphia, where Edie's grandparents lived.

As a child, Edie was a voracious reader and loved to write. She also played the piano from the time she was seven years old and adored singing. When she was six, her parents divorced. In retrospect, Edie understands that they hardly knew each other when they married and came from such diverse backgrounds; but at the time, she was devastated. Her mother went to work as a bookkeeper to support Edie and her little sister and remarried soon after the divorce; her stepfather, who worked for the federal government, adopted her and she took his name. Edie's mother asked her not to tell anyone who her real father was, but she told her friends anyway; her mother was furious about that.

Edie's relationship with her mother was complicated, like many mother-daughter relationships. As the only natural parent present in her life, her mother was her world, and of course, Edie loved her. But her mother was also a tough woman and very rigid, which Edie hated.

On her first day of high school, Edie discovered the harp and immediately began taking lessons, setting her sights on being a concert harpist. Her mother couldn't understand her obsession with music and the harp, but she was proud of her at recitals and for winning a Board of Education music scholarship when she graduated from high school.

The teenage years were rough, because Edie held on to many resentments: that she had to keep the secret about her real father, that she had been given a new name of the man who was raising her, and that she was not allowed any contact with her biological father. What saved her was her passion for the harp and classical music. Practicing four to six hours a day kept her from having to deal with differences with her mother, in particular.

When she left home at eighteen, she began searching for her father in phone books from all over the country. She hunted on and off for him her entire life and didn't meet him face to face until she was forty-five years old. Living in the desert near Death Valley, California, he had remarried and had three children. They had a grand reunion on Valentine's Day 1990, and were very close until his death three years later.

It was only after she met her biological father that she came to fully appreciate that her stepfather who raised her was far more stable than her natural father. Fortunately, her stepfather was still alive, so she was able to tell him that she had come to recognize that he—and not her other father—was, in fact, her "real" father and to thank him for being there for her all those years. Looking for her father for most of her life, she believes, led her to marry two men who are each much older than she. Her first husband is eleven years her senior and her second husband, thirteen years.

According to Edie, her relationship with her mother "fluctuated between being okay and God-awful" through her twenties and thirties. By the time she hit her forties and fifties, they had worked through most of their issues and chose to put down their weapons and forgive and love each other. Her mother turned ninety-three this year, and now Edie is grateful that they've been afforded all the years they needed to heal their relationship.

Edie continued playing the harp into college but after her sophomore year, could no longer support herself, take lessons, and keep up the pace of practicing, studying, and going to class. With deep regret, she left her harp—and her heart—behind. For the next twenty-eight years, she taught music but never touched the harp. She would not allow herself to listen to the harp or think about it—the longing was too painful.

Then in the early 1990s, three people close to her died within eight months of each other. While coping with this tremendous loss, she started thinking about her own mortality and why she put off things she truly loved. She knew that she had to go back to the harp.

With money left to her by one of her friends, she bought a harp and started taking lessons. As she used the harp to help her grieve from the triple loss, she realized personally the healing properties of the harp and decided to become certified to play the harp in medical facilities.

In 2002, Edie founded Bedside Harp, which offers patients comfort, a release of emotions, and relaxation through harp therapy. She has played for people through their births and deaths and every kind of illness in between, beginning with her own husband who was on life support.

In a poignant telling of her own story, Edie Elkan, sixty-five, shares the details of a dream lost and found, and a life that she created to live out that vision. Today she is thrilled to have reached the point of being able to say, "I am becoming the person I always wanted to be."

In her own words....

My first day in high school I discovered the concert harp. I was looking for a classroom and somehow wound up in the music department, peeked into a practice room and saw a harp for the first time up close. I knew from the very first sight of it that I had to play this instrument. I told my family that night that I would be taking harp lessons. A harp costs the same as a car, and I didn't come from a wealthy family. My family's philosophy was, if there was something you really wanted to do, figure out how to do it; so I started babysitting. Every dollar I earned went to renting a harp or buying strings.

I went to the Philadelphia Musical Academy, now the University of the Arts, and studied with the first harpist of the Philadelphia Orchestra. With a double major in music education and harp performance, there was little time for anything. Practicing four to six hours a day all through high school and two years of college, I ate, drank, and lived music, and loved every minute of it.

After two and a half years of college, I burned out. At that time, there were no part-time or evening school options, so I dropped out of school and got a job, giving up the harp, along with my dream to become a concert harpist. It was devastating. But I couldn't afford it any longer, nor could I keep up the pace.

At twenty years old, I worked fulltime in business, had my own apartment and tried to make the best of things. I fell in love with a fascinating archaeology student pursuing his master's degree from the University of Pennsylvania. Only problem was that he was an Arab, and I was raised Jewish. History repeated itself—my mother married out of her clan, but I went one step beyond and followed my fiancé to Jordan, marrying him as soon as I arrived and living there for three years. My last year and a half there, I taught music at the American Community School in Amman. It was one of my all-time favorite jobs, but it was during a very scary period; I was over there during the '67 war and I was on the side that lost.

After three years, we came back to the states where we had our daughter, and he began doctoral studies in Chicago. When our daughter was two, I went back to work. Four years later, my husband got his Ph.D. and wanted to go back to Jordan to live. We had our challenges in this marriage, and I didn't want to go with him; ultimately we divorced but we remain friends to this day.

Chicago is where they make the finest concert harps in the world, and I lived in the neighborhood of the biggest showroom, but I never allowed myself to go in. I did everything to avoid thinking about the harp. I was barely eking out a living. I didn't realize at the time how present the harp was in my mind. Even so, I never once went to the showroom. I went to orchestra concerts but never looked in the direction of the harp. I couldn't bear to hear the sound of the harp—it was too painful for me. I didn't realize until many years later that I longed for the harp my whole adult life.

I always played the piano, but I didn't have the same feeling about it as I had about the harp. When you play a piano, you touch the key, which releases the damper and a hammer strikes the string, which makes the sound. With the harp, you take your bare finger and pluck the string. It's a more personal encounter. And you hold it next to your heart; you hold it in your arms as if you're hugging it in order to play it, and then you feel the vibration instantly, because it's up against your chest. It's a very intimate, healing instrument.

Our bodies are 60-70% water. When there's a vibration, you see the ripples in the water. That's what going on inside of you when you play the harp; the vibrations go right through you. And the harp's timbre — the soothing, gentle tones for which the instrument is so well loved — makes it apparent why this instrument is so often referred to not just as a harp, but rather, as a healing harp.

After my divorce, I came back to Philadelphia because my family was here, and I raised my daughter here. She is my heart; she has taught me more about love and life than anyone else. While she doesn't play an instrument now (she played the piano and flute briefly as a child), she applies her creative nature to technology (she has a degree in Information Technology Systems). She also has an artist's eye for design, which she expresses in her clothing and home decor. And she is a rather amazing ballroom dancer. Her childhood was complicated as well, having gone through the separation and divorce of her father and me at the tender age of four and then my remarriage when she was ten. Unlike me, though, she got to see her father as she grew up, and I've encouraged her relationship with her stepmother and half-siblings. I applaud the choices she's made in her life, especially because they've been different from mine.

I was a single mom for six years, and then met my second husband in 1979. We married in 1980, when I became stepmother to his three children, two of whom were adults by then. During my single years, I'd worked for Globe Security Systems climbing my way up the corporate ladder from executive secretary to corporate compliance manager, becoming the first female in the company to achieve higher management status.

My job was demanding and required a great deal of traveling, which infringed on my home life. When I was single, I didn't have much choice; but after my remarriage, my subsistence no longer depended on my working, so in 1982, I quit my job in business to be a fulltime wife and mom. By then the kids were mostly grown, so after painting the house and completing a couple of knitting and sewing projects, I realized I needed something more in my life. That's when I went back to school at the community college and earned an Associate of Arts degree. From there I went on to get a BA in non-fiction writing at University of Pennsylvania, all the while teaching piano, putting on recitals, and keeping the home fires burning. Things were good—my life had balance and meaning, but I had still not found my bliss.

Then, between 1992 and 1993, three people who were important in my life died within eight months of each other: my mentor and dear friend, whom I known since high school; my biological father; and another close friend. I was the chief caregiver of both friends and also executor of their estates and needed to give up my life to take care of their complex affairs. I was so busy working on their portfolios that I didn't give myself the time to grieve fully for their deaths. One died, then next one, and the next and then I had to handle properties and possessions, protect investments, and oversee a myriad of legal and accounting matters. These were things I didn't want to do, but my two friends had trusted me to carry out their last wishes; so, of course, I dedicated myself to doing that and was so devoted to taking care of their businesses, in fact, that I put my own emotions on the back burner.

A year after they died, I went to a grief counselor and told her that I couldn't cry. Everything was blocked. I said, "I know that I have a great deal of mourning to do, and I don't know where it is inside." We had one session. At end, the counselor said to me, "What can you do to bring joy back to your life?" I said, "Joy? I'm not talking joy, I need to *feel* again." I couldn't give her an answer. I went to my car, put the key in the ignition, and before I turned it on, I knew I had to return to the harp. I knew I had to take the money that my friend had left me and sink it into buying a concert harp. I was recapturing a lost dream.

When you're smacked in the face with so many deaths that happen within a short period of time, you begin to think differently about life. I hadn't touched the harp in twenty-eight years, but I knew in my gut that this is what I needed to do. My husband encouraged me. He said, "Life is so fragile. You keep putting off what you want to do. You'll die without having done it. If this is what you want to do, then do it."

I located my first harp teacher and paid for her trip to Chicago, so we could go to the harp factory that I had avoided when I lived there. We picked out a harp, and I came back and wrote to the first harpist of Philadelphia Orchestra who graciously took me on as a student. I studied with her for six years until 2002. During this time, I saw what other people were saying: the harp *is* a healing instrument. It's mentioned in the Bible in that context. I started thinking about how I had used it to heal myself during my stormy teenage years, and now all these years later, it was helping me to grieve. I went to California to get certified to play the harp in medical facilities. I had taught music my entire life, and now I had the credentials to work as a harp therapist on my own, but I realized that what I *really* wanted to do was to create a program to train and inspire others to do this amazing work; to my mind, the best way to do that would be to partner with a medical facility.

I conceived of the idea of forming a school that would work out of such a facility where my students and I would play for patients, where I could teach folks the harp for self-healing, and train and certify harpists to play in health care. I had not initially imagined that such a facility would be a hospital—I figured it would be a life-care facility that would consist of independent residents, assisted living residents, nursing home residents, and perhaps, hospice patients as well. I played hundreds of volunteer hours at such facilities hoping to convince them to partner with me, but I couldn't find a facility to sign on, even though they all loved the idea.

In 2001 my husband went in the hospital for double knee replacement surgery. A week later he was on life support; he had monitors on every part of his body. They had accidentally given him two incompatible antibiotics, and he nearly lost his life. In midst of this horror, it occurred to me to bring my small harp to the hospital, but the hospital staff was against it. They said I couldn't bring in a harp, that they didn't want any music in the Surgical ICU. I insisted: "I'm going to play for my husband. I've played at the bedside of strangers. You can close the door, but I'm playing."

I started playing. The staff came rushing in after about five minutes into my playing and said, "*What are you doing?* All of his vital signs are in the normal range."

I said, "I am playing love songs for my husband."

They said, "Keep playing and play for everyone." I came every day with my harp and after seven days, my husband turned the corner and left the SICU. When I played, patients and staff would hang out in his room; the nurses brought in people in wheel chairs and walkers.

That's how I realized: Oh, my God! That's what I need to do—run a harp therapy program out of a hospital. The first hospital that signed on was Robert Wood Johnson Hospital in Hamilton, New Jersey, where, a month after 9-11, the anthrax-infected postal employees were being treated. Seeing how patients and staff immediately responded to the gentle sounds of my little harp, they told me to create whatever program I wanted, so I created Bedside Harp in 2002. Now Bedside Harp is partnered with five hospitals in New Jersey and Pennsylvania. Our certification program is college based; we've taught nearly six hundred people who never played the harp before to play for their own healing and have certified sixty harp therapists from all over the country.

Along the way I got a master's degree in liberal arts in 2007. Every day we are truly making a notable difference in health care. I limit the number of hospitals we're in, because I don't want to overextend myself. We could be much bigger, but I'd not be able to offer hands-on supervision and mentoring. I personally play two to four days a week in our host hospitals, so that I'm at every hospital at least every other week. I promised myself that I'd always keep playing for patients and that's the core of what I do. I can always hire people to do the paper work.

Bedside Harp is the gift that keeps giving. People I trained the earliest are now training others. I had no idea how many people wanted to play this instrument. The harp is a very different kind of instrument; you can see it in a person's eyes when they first hear it. In my wildest dreams I could never have imagined that we'd have taught so many people to play the harp.

For almost thirty years, I avoided the harp. I'd listen to classical guitar—a lot of classical guitar—because I wouldn't or *couldn't* go near the sound of a harp. The sound of the guitar was the closest I could get to it. When I went back to the harp, it was like coming home. It was like picking up a piece of myself that I had left behind. I had given up all hope. It was wild! My journey with the harp was unfinished and undone. I longed for it in a passive way. I didn't even let myself know how much I longed for it.

A theme of my life has been to never give up hope, to hold on to your dreams. I longed to come face to face with my lost father for all those years, and I did much the same with the harp. When I finally got to meet him and too, when I went back to playing the harp again, it was Christmas two thousand times.

Until you're dead, it's never too late to follow your dreams. Allow yourself to go after the things you long for or you'll die never having done them. There will be naysayers. When I first got the idea to run a program out of a hospital, my sister said to me, "You're going to walk around the hospital and play the harp? Who would want that?" Well, it turns out, over forty-four thousand, five hundred patients and counting want that—that's the number of one-on-one sessions we've documented since I started Bedside Harp. Even if someone tries to rain on your parade, you have to follow your dream. If you make a difference in one person's life—and that includes your own—it all will have been well worth it.

Rediscovering the harp was an act of honoring and synthesizing all that came before and all that really matters to me. The dots representing my earlier experiences once seemed to be scattered about, hither and yon; coming home to myself involved my understanding how each is an important piece of a unified, meaningful whole. The places I'd been, the people I'd known, the life I led as a child, a teen, in my twenties, thirties and forties form the essence of who I am as much as they gave me the skills, confidence and courage to make my dearest dreams come true. I founded an innovative business, developed and launched unique educational programs, kept learning new things, and inspired and empowered those who looked to me for guidance. And, perhaps above all, I've blessed patients and staff by offering them music from my heart.

Elaine Pinkerton

Adopting a New Attitude

In the aftermath of World War II, a troubled college student gave her five-year-old daughter Elaine and her two-year-old son to her psychology professor and his wife after the children had spent time in abusive foster care. The student gave up her children because she didn't have the means to feed or clothe them and knew she didn't have the emotional stamina to be a good mother. Elaine, however, suspected this was not the true reason her mother abandoned her. She believed it was really her fault: she wasn't good enough. If she weren't to blame, then her mother must be a monster to give away her children; that thought was intolerable.

The move to the professor's home transformed Elaine's life. She had loving parents, Richard and Reva, who were proud of her; she had plenty to eat, her own bicycle, and shelves and shelves of books to read.

But there was a stigma attached to adoption in those days. No one talked about it. The secrecy surrounding her birth parents and her first five years, and the fact that she was adopted created a disturbing undercurrent in Elaine's life. She told me, "Even with all I had, I was afraid of being sent back or not being good enough. They didn't make me feel this way, but I felt I had to be Little Miss Perfect."

Her adoptive parents didn't talk about why they adopted her or when her real parents would come back for her. As she grew older and they didn't return for her, Elaine's fears were confirmed: she wasn't pretty enough or smart enough. This shameful secret stayed with her for years.

When she was eleven, Elaine received a five-year diary with a red plastic cover for Christmas. It had a lock and key so she could write anything she wanted, and no one would ever know. That diary became her best friend. She wrote down everything that happened to her, everything she felt, and everything she worried about. But mostly, she poured out her heart about her shameful secret. Her diary never judged or disapproved. She could say anything. And she did, every day in diary after diary. She continued to keep diaries through her teen years and college, while she was a wife and mother, and even later, as a grandmother.

Today she houses those diaries in row upon row of a five-foot bookshelf in her writing room. The spine of each book bears the year it was written. They range from 1954 to the present. Behind the bookshelf, a window looks out on the labyrinth she has built, which she walks every day.

For her first fifty-five years—even though she completed graduate school, survived two marriages, raised two sons, published four books, and ran nine marathons—Elaine never felt good enough. If you met her, you'd never know she felt so bad about herself. She is a vibrant, attractive woman who looks a lot younger than her sixty-six years. She has shoulder length blond hair in a pageboy with bangs, a ready smile and self-effacing humor.

But the fact is, her shameful secret was eating her up inside. She was haunted by fears of rejection, abandonment and powerlessness. She admits to making some bad choices: tolerating a punishing job, gravitating to the wrong men, and then believing that she couldn't exist without having a man to validate her. Those early-sown seeds of loss had grown into poisonous plants that she'd eaten for so many years that she could not imagine another way of existing.

A few years ago, a strange thing happened. Shortly after her second husband died, she decided to read her diaries, with the intention of destroying them before her children and grandchildren read them. She had lost three parents and a husband in just a few years and didn't know where she was going. She thought that if she figured out *who* she had been and *where* she had been it might help her decide where to go from here. She might even write about her adoption, she thought, since it was now so far in the past. As she read page after page, it slowly dawned on her that there was nothing so special about her own personal story. "Everyone has something. Mine was that my mother left me," she told me. "I was affected by that my whole life, but I don't have to be affected any more. I can be me and feel that it's enough."

This was a huge revelation for her and one that influenced every aspect of her life from then on. Harvesting the diaries—reading and analyzing them—became her life's work. She is in the process of writing a book, called *Diary of a Goodbye Baby,* which resulted from this intensive self-study. The understanding she received, she hopes, will help others who've been adopted or who adopted children.

This is her fifth book. Besides two guidebooks to Santa Fe, Elaine wrote *From Calcutta with Love,* the story of her adopted parents' long-distance love affair while her father was stationed in India during World War II, told through their letters, and *Beast of Bengal,* a mystery based in an American military hospital in Calcutta also during World War II.

In the next section, Elaine Pinkerton talks about the journey that led her to read her diaries, the internal transformations that occurred, and the changes in her life as a result. She also speaks about how she was able to abandon her "Poor Me" attitude to acknowledge herself as a strong, wise woman, a woman who now accepts the hand she has been dealt and taught herself to live a life filled with gratitude.

In her own words....

I'm writing the kind of book I wish I had when I was growing up adopted. My birth mother is still alive, though we're not close; my wonderful adoptive parents are gone. So why shouldn't I tell the story? I started to tell it years ago and called it "Reunion." It was to be about my reunion with my birth mother and father, but that book never happened. This book is about my reunion with myself. I'm much stronger than I've ever given myself credit for. I'm realizing that *I am enough*. I'm open to having a partner, but I'm not on a quest. If the love of my life doesn't enter, so be it. I'm blessed that every day is my own.

But I must say, it took me a long time to get here. I don't really want to talk about the foster homes I was in the first five years. Let's just say I was abused and leave it at that.

My years with Richard and Reva were happy years. I felt wanted, I had friends, I was surrounded by books, and they were proud of my brother and me. We were given lots of advantages. But there was a disgrace then about not having one's own children. Remember this was the Fifties. My parents avoided the topic of adoption; they said they wanted me to think of them as my real parents. I was much taller and more vigorous and rambunctious than they were. They were more petite. I remember the excruciating perms my mother gave me in fifth grade. Before that I looked dorky in braids. I was painfully self-conscious, because I felt I had to wear a mask, because I had to be the real daughter. A lot of it was the times and the reticence of my well-meaning parents.

When I was five, just after being adopted, I'd ask a question like, whose tummy did I grow in? I could never get a straight answer. Mother would get all teary-eyed and she'd say, "You're our real daughter." I never talked to my father about being adopted; I didn't want to anger him or fall out of favor. There was a big disconnect. It took me years to work it out. I felt bad about bringing up the topic, but I did. Mother always seemed hurt when I asked questions.

Everything was so much better in my "new" life, but the burning questions festered and took on a life of their own. I was just not okay; otherwise how could my mother have given me away? Underneath it all, I never felt secure. I knew there was something missing, but I had never heard of other adopted children, so I didn't know what it was.

Yet it wasn't the time to talk about those things, and my parents didn't want it flapping about our town that they couldn't have their own children. People kept a lot of secrets in the Fifties that were harmful.

I do have wonderful memories of growing up in West Virginia and then in North Carolina, where we were on our bikes all summer. It was neat to be a professor's daughter. My father was my role model and my inspiration, especially because he was so literate, and I wanted to be a writer. He had a book program on educational TV, and my friend and I got to be on TV talking about books. When I was a sophomore, we moved to Virginia as he climbed the academic ladder.

During the teen years, I had a breakdown in communications with my parents. That came after my mother read my diary. (She said she found it when she was cleaning my room!) I felt so humiliated and ashamed when she brought it up at the dinner table. It was like I was wearing a big scarlet A. I always related to my father more. I'd come home from a date and talk to my father about books until two in the morning.

As a teen, there was a lot of chasing around with my girl friends, calling boys on the phone. I'd do sneaky things like I'd come home from a date and slink out again. That's when the diary writing was stepped up! My friends and I were all boy crazy.

In those days, you had to get your M-R-S or you were called a spinster. I was a Woodrow Wilson fellowship finalist to Stanford, the only woman among seven men. I was a leader, but my parents only wanted to marry me off. They wouldn't send me to Stanford. Instead I went to Mary Washington, then lived at home and went to the University of Virginia. I taught for a year in Alabama and then got a master's.

That's where I fell in love for the first time. I didn't know my mind, so I married unwisely. I should have married Hugh, a poet who adored me. Along came Jack (not his real name), a doctor. We were married in 1966 and lived in Iran for four years while we both worked for the CIA. I was a secretary (that was my cover). Mostly I did Xeroxing for the Boy Scouts, and my first son was born there.

When we came back, things went downhill. Jack found he loved his receptionist, never mind that they were both married to other people. I was devastated. That's when I embraced running; he couldn't stand it. I stayed with him for the children, but I stayed in the marriage too long. If he hadn't found someone else, I would have. There had to be a way out. I knew I didn't want to spend another fifteen years like this. I'd rather die than face that. We probably shouldn't have gotten married in the first place. We divorced in 1980 when my sons were seven and nine. I was a single parent for eleven years.

Then I married Wesley, who was twenty-one years older than I. We were together another eighteen years. He died four years ago, and it took four years for my re-emergence after his death. There are so many single women here leading rich lives. It doesn't matter that you're solo. You wake up and the whole day is yours. I'm not holding anything up for a man. If it happens, it will.

Both husbands discouraged my writing. Jack, the first one, told me I just didn't have it. He wanted a snazzier wife, a thinner wife. He thought I was too fat. One horrible image comes back: I'm in Lamaze breathing classes, on all fours. He told me I looked like Sally, our dog. When I came home with the baby, I was flooded with maternal emotions and caught up with nursing. I remember Jack was away on a trip; he gave me *The Story of O* to read while he was gone. He wanted me to get over it.

He wanted a satellite to himself, and he wouldn't even acknowledge my writing. He thought right off the bat I should be Hemingway or Faulkner and be successful and make lots of money. I felt like I was a master baker, and he wouldn't take a bite of my cake. It was one more instance of my not being good enough. If only I had been thin enough.... Oh, I don't know. I wasn't what he wanted. I looked like I'd be the right wife from the outside, but he didn't like what was inside.

The good thing about single parenthood was that I was writing and running marathons; but on the negative side, I wasn't a good parent. I was so concerned about making a living. I was replicating what my birth mother did, and she didn't do it very well. I know she did the best she could. I was working at Los Alamos labs as a writer and editor and had a radio program. I had two different partners for about three years each. Men easily sidetracked me....

For years I knew there was a stash of letters from my parents to each other while Daddy was stationed in India during World War II, but the letters weren't that important to me. After my divorce, I became interested in these letters. My dream was to help my father write a book about his experiences. But when I went back to talk to him about the project, he had Alzheimer's disease: He was there physically but mentally he was gone. It was so heartbreaking to see him. I called him my daddy look-alike. He looked like my father, but there was nothing there. The poor soul would wander around, get dressed up to teach at the university, and he hadn't taught in ten years! One bittersweet, funny scene: he took me to the nursing station in the ward and introduced me, like he was introducing me to his colleagues at the university.

We had such a close bond. For years and years, we'd write each other letters every Sunday afternoon. His became complete non-sequiturs, and then he'd write shorter letters, then my mother started writing them for him. I felt abandoned all over again. You start as an orphan, you have this wonderful parent and life becomes so much better. He was in the world and then suddenly he was not. I was back to Square One.

I quit my day job to read the letters. It hit me: we don't have forever. I started reading and thinking about my parents' relationship. I loved reading their correspondence. I'd sit under the cherry tree at a small table in my backyard and read them every single day. There were so many letters; it was challenging to choose which to publish. When my mother was going down hill, I stepped up my efforts to find a publisher. Texas Tech published *From Calcutta with Love* in 2006.

I got to thinking: Every time I have a book published, someone leaves me. My mother got to see the book as she was dying. It was my farewell present to her; I feel good about that. It meant so much to her to have it. I was going to see her one more time, but I had a book signing for Valentine's Day. I stayed for the book signing, and she slipped away. It took me a long time to forgive myself. The hospice worker said it's easier for people not to be there. At least my mother got to see the book.

From Calcutta with Love is a love story on many levels: I canonized my parents. It was my tribute to them, my love for them, and it was also an old-fashioned love story between them. Dad was stuck in India and had to write her a letter every day.

I was not aware of my parents' passionate feelings for each other while I was growing up. Well, there was no passion allowed; it was really strange. I'm sure there was passion there, but it was subtle. He placed her on a pedestal. I didn't like to think of something sexual between my parents—no one does! When she read the letters later, she picked up the passion. I came to a place of love with them. The way they weren't wonderful: they had an inability to talk about anything, like my abuse in foster care. They thought if they discussed it, I'd dwell on it. The fact that I was adopted was a burden I had to carry with me and hide. They didn't want my cover blown.

Four years ago, after my second husband died, I didn't know what to do with myself. My diaries felt like an albatross. I thought there must be something shameful and embarrassing about them, so I avoided reading them. I thought I'd throw some of them away or destroy them before my grandchildren saw them, because some years of my first marriage were very rough. My then-husband didn't pay any attention to me; I imagined that he was cheating on me even though I had no proof. After I read about those years, I tore them up and scattered the pages; it was quite satisfying. Now if I throw the rest of them away, it won't bother me.

Reading those diaries, I was reminded of how much I wanted to have a relationship with Velma, my birth mother, as an adult. I waited thirty-eight years before meeting her, having last seen her when I was five years old. Fear kept me from aggressively searching for her. First, I did not want to hurt the feelings of my adoptive parents. When my first husband voted against the idea, I reluctantly decided that he was right. His words were something like, "We don't want to end up with her on our doorstep."

Years passed. Life was complicated enough without adding another set of relatives, people I might not even like. However, my unanswered questions weighed heavily. What health issues might be at stake? Did breast cancer or osteoporosis run in the family? What was my genetic inheritance? How was I like my birth mother? When she contacted me in the early 1980s, I went to California to meet her. In many ways it was a good meeting. The missing puzzle pieces fell into place. I learned the real story about how I came about—the madcap World War II romance between my birth mother and birth father, health questions answered, why she felt she had to give me up.

But then she disappeared again, and I felt abandoned all over again. She couldn't relate to me. She was also sort of jealous of me; she wasn't happy at my success. My first book had just come out when she came here to visit. It was so thrilling to me, but she didn't like the fact that people received it well. She felt I should have paid more attention to *her*. She said, "You're just too busy." That's the same attitude my first husband had about my writing.

Looking at our relationship in retrospect, I feel that our reunions were not entirely bad. I've decided to let go of my disappointment and adopt the attitude of "It is what it is."

Going through the journals, my feelings about myself began to shift. It first occurred to me that I wasn't so unique when I read aloud from my diary during a program of Dear Diary Readings with other people. Five of us read from our teenage diaries. Everyone had a different version of the same thing as a teenager. I wasn't the only one whose mother had read her diary!

As I read my journals, I wept at certain scenes. One day, the fourth of July, my mother made this incredible lunch for me, and I told her I was too busy to eat. I cried and cried when I read that. I wanted to put my arms around her and say, "Please forgive me." She tried hard. She'd take me shopping and buy me clothes. The last five years of her life we talked every day. I didn't understand or appreciate her until I read the World War II letters. Once I had more data, I wanted to step inside my parents' lives, especially when he came back from the war.

That's why reading *my* diaries was transformational for me. I feel very fortunate that I did that. Having more information made me, in retrospect, realize how my life really was and how hard I tried.... I really admire the fact that I was such a survivor. I was a single parent, working full time, training for marathons running up to fifteen miles a day. Instead of thinking how pathetic I was, I could now admire what I did. If I had the energy to survive that—and I did— there's a lot there.

I gained a new respect for myself. I didn't have to keep going back to the same broken-record of "Poor me, I'm adopted." It turned around how I feel about myself. Even though I had judged myself harshly in the past and didn't do as well as I would have liked, I admire myself now. I had to reach back and symbolically put my arms around myself. I wept at things I did, like trying blindly to make a relationship work that couldn't possibly. The persistence and determination that allowed me to run in nine marathons and take an hour and a half off my time has served me well. This is somebody who really has a lot of inner strength and courage, as well as huge blind spots, of course.

I didn't know what was in those diaries until I went back and read them. I knew I was looking for a thread: about the adopted me. But now there's another me that's wiser, richer, and better. You made stupid choices. So? That was then. So you were adopted? A lot of people have something that happened to them. You move on. I have a wider lens now.

Before I finished reading the diaries, I started the discipline of gratitude. I've decided not to waste time with negative energy; I close the door to that. After my husband died, I built a labyrinth in the back yard. As I walk it, I say to myself: "Things are as they are, and my happiness or unhappiness depends on my actions and not on an outside source."

Another thing I do is commemorate the things that are good or the things I like about myself: my health, my sons, my daughters-in-law, my granddaughters, my friends, my house, my work as a librarian, my writing. Yes, I count my blessings.

I also have a way of checking myself so I don't get into a slump when the monster inside says, "This sucks: you're alone looking at a beautiful sunset." Instead I ask, what is my relationship to the present moment? If I keep gratitude in mind, I stay in the present and don't assume that I'm going to have a horrible time. I have to shake that dark side and ask, who's in control here? I don't succeed all the time, but I'm moving in the right direction.

Reading in my diaries about small things in the past, like the golden light on an autumn afternoon or the snow falling on a winter day, made me more present now. These beautiful descriptions meant I was appreciating the place in which I live. I still live in the same place, and I still have that same young spirit. There was good then as now; like a wild flower seed, it can sprout and bloom years later. It was always there— through bad relationships and tedious jobs. It gives life continuity.

I just enjoy being. I didn't know what to do with this house after my second husband died. I hated the yard. I went to a day camp for writers, where I got the idea to build the labyrinth. Now I love the yard. I sit and breathe after I walk the labyrinth. I'm sort of a pantheist; I love being in nature. It's transformational. I allow myself to simply be. I'm not as hard on myself. I'm more patient with myself, and more philosophical. I can relate to people more authentically. This has happened because I've gotten away from being Ms. Perfect. That's been a real gift of harvesting these journals. No one's keeping score. I don't have to please my inner parent any more.

It's been a fascinating journey. I'm much more excited about life. I'm getting over myself. It's good to grieve but not too much and not too little either. I know now that much of my former depression resulted from unresolved grief. Once I faced the grief and recognized how badly it served me, I was able to tame it. I'd watch the parade of my thoughts, letting it have its time on the stage, letting it consume me. But I don't let it get the better of me. I'll say to my grief: "Oh, *you're* here again." I'll write about it; that helps a lot. You won't do away with grief: to grieve is to be human.

I feel grateful for being in this place on the planet for all these years. It's a sense of still being me. I was moved by those descriptions in my diaries, and they brought back good memories. It was a treat to read about my impressions of nature then. Nature is my therapy. When I was out there running, that was my job. Now when I can be outside, it's a gift to myself. The descriptions were bittersweet: Those moments are gone forever but I'm so glad I took the time to describe them. It's a luminous world.

Cinny Green

Journey into Wilderness

Some women love the feminine. As little girls, they adore wearing pink and purple, trying new clothes on their dolls and playing dress-up. As they become teenagers, they have their wedding planned down to the color-coordinated after-dinner mints. Cinny Green was not one of those girls. She was a tomboy who loved to play "Capture the Flag" and Cowboys and Indians with the boys in her neighborhood. She wasn't interested in sitting around with the girls and their Barbies. As she got older, she put on a few pounds and felt uncomfortable with her body; she wasn't sure where she fit in. It took several turning points over the course of her lifetime —childbirth, divorce, coming out as a lesbian and her discovery of the wilderness—to give her a true sense of identity, which brought her home to her authentic self at age sixty.

Cinny, who is a writer and editor, and her brother grew up in Worcester, Massachusetts. When she was twelve, her family moved to Puebla, a beautiful colonial city east of Mexico City, for her father's job at Norton Abrasives, a Fortune 500 company. He was a mid-level executive there for most of his life until he became vice president. Cinny went to school in Mexico for two years and then came back to the states to go to boarding school for high school. Her parents moved to Italy briefly and then settled back in Massachusetts.

Her mother, a Southern belle from Arkansas, was active in the Junior League and very invested in being the wife of a successful man. Surprisingly, her parents were liberals politically in a conservative community. Cinny remembers with pride that her mother believed strongly in a woman's right to choose and in the Seventies in the heat of Roe vs. Wade, she linked arms with young girls and marched them into Planned Parenthood for counseling. Later in her life, her mother developed a drinking problem that the family never confronted.

Some of Cinny's fondest childhood memories occurred at her grandparents' homes. At their retirement farm near the Berkshires she loved to walk in the woods, ski, ride horseback and swim in the summer. Cinny also enjoyed visiting her great grandparents' beautiful rural cabins in Marshfield, Massachusetts, a place they had built after returning from South India, where they were missionaries for many years.

Cinny went to Lake Forest College, where she met her husband, a bright, funny iconoclastic guy. Upon graduation, they embarked on teaching jobs, first in classrooms on the prairie of North Dakota, then in Florida and Virginia. While teaching, they bought eighty acres of land near Madison, Wisconsin, so they could become homesteaders. Cinny wanted to recreate the warm, cozy feeling she had experienced on her grandparents' land. The following year they moved there, and that's where they raised their two daughters. They also grew organic produce and did wood working.

While they were developing the farm, Cinny was also creating a life for herself outside it: As she taught dyslexic and gifted and talented children, the community began to recognize her for her teaching skills. Her husband couldn't find his footing. He lost his passion for farming and woodworking, just as she was beginning to feel confident, competent and respected as a teacher. When they continued to grow apart, Cinny left him. They divorced and shared custody of their daughters for the next five years.

Thrown into the dating scene after her divorce, Cinny dated men and women. She fell in love with Maureen, an illustrator and graphic designer who has been her partner for the last thirteen years. They decided to leave Madison and move west to New Mexico, where the landscape reminded Cinny of her early years in Mexico, and the atmosphere was more nurturing of artists.

Three years ago, Cinny and Maureen added a Rottweiler to their household. Walking her around the neighborhood awakened something in Cinny: It brought back her childhood love of animals and her passion for the outdoors. The more she walked, the more she yearned to take longer and longer hikes, eventually leading to expansive treks into the wilderness, both here and abroad. By journeying into the wilderness, Cinny Green has found her deepest self and her true home. She shares her thoughts about this in the following section and in her new book, *Trail Writer's Guide,* which explores the connection between wilderness, moving our bodies and creativity.

In her own words....

In my family history, we have many generations of people who have journeyed all over the world and lived in many places. My sense of family is grounded in this desire to move and be out in the world. Family is or can be a home, but that sense of home as a very distinct, long-term location is not what home means to me. I've changed my own home so many times that I define it more as where we are as a collective–a family of ownership, my married family, and now my present partnership. It's really the current adventure I'm embarking on. I have tried to recreate family and place a number of times and what I've come to is that it's really important to be in a place but not at the expense of a journey.

I discovered the wilderness three years ago when I got a big dog that needed walking. I started going out in the hills around town. Lo and behold— it's beautiful. Now the dog stays home and I go walking! I had always walked for pleasure, of course, but not into the wilderness. Physically, the journey is more challenging, and the payoff is greater, especially when you stay there for a while. My sense of home as journey into the wilderness is not a great departure from my sense of home—the place—being part of extended journeys to different places too.

This might sound like a contradiction but it's not, given my history. Being in the last third of my life, I've come to this place of embracing the fact that I can have a home, *and* a sense of journey, *and* the actual journey. They're all nourishing and all provide the kind of definition of what home is supposed to do for you: a sense of identity, a sense of self, and a place to go when you need to be embraced. At times of my life they have been contradictory but not now. Now they are different sides of the same coin.

The process of getting into back country started on my fifty-eighth birthday when my partner and I hiked and camped outside of Pagosa Springs, Colorado. We were hiking up to Windy Pass near Wolf Creek. It was very steep—a two-thousand foot elevation gain in three miles. It was very hard for me; I wasn't in terrific shape. Maureen, who's twenty years younger, was way ahead of me; the dog was running around. I was feeling very discouraged. Feeling my age. Down on myself about struggling to get up to the destination.

I finally got up there, and it was so beautiful: the layers of the mountains, the paths through them, the expanse of sky. In spite of the struggle of getting there, I just wanted to keep going. I burst into tears and in that instant knew that this was something I wanted to do for the rest of my life: I wanted to keep going on those trails.

Since then I've been working to make that happen. I'm getting fitter. It's no longer about giving the dog exercise. It's about me getting where I want to go. I have different levels of training. I walk my dogs every day for an hour (we have another dog as well). I started taking spinning classes; that took me to another level. I try to do that three times a week. I visualize exactly what trail I'm on while I'm spinning.

I've added snowshoeing to my repertoire, I've become a Sierra Club hike leader, and I try to do trail work once a week. Every season, I take an overnight trip: a one-hundred-mile walk from Santa Fe to Taos, two hundred miles in Scotland, walking ten to twenty miles a day while I was there. I'm just realizing how much my body loves to do that. Not fast, just being able to walk every day. It feels so good. I feel a call to do it.

The lesson is to keep moving. You keep moving, and you can do it. You don't have to go fast or get there first. I do feel a sense of urgency because I'm realistic about my age. Probably this level of physical activity has a finite time frame. I'm starting late in life. Now I'll do grander journeys into the wilderness, but they need to be done in the next ten years or so.

For the first time in years, I'm comfortable with my body. I was a chunky little girl though I outgrew it as an adolescent. But that early image of myself as a chubby kid stayed with me, though I was always a tomboy. It didn't help that my family (of origin) had a negative association with chunkiness. My weight would go up and down. When I hit menopause, I put on about twenty pounds. It was the dickens to get off. I took some off when I started hiking but it took awhile. Spinning is what got it off.

Now I'm back to the comfortable body weight I had in college, and I'm the most fit I've ever been. In terms of endurance, I'm at the best too. I'd be exhausted going up the mountain, but once I got to the top, I could go for miles. I could do the Continental Divide Trail now.

You can get more fit at sixty. People don't believe that about themselves, and it keeps them from trying. I'm putting together a walking book for the people I work for. People think that they need enormous amounts of discipline, but it's really just a small shift in their thinking to get them outside to get in shape. I'm working on expressing that and creating a program so people can think differently about exercise and feel the difference.

When I think back on my life, there were several turning points that brought me to where I am today. Childbirth was the first. I had grown up with a negative view of womanhood, because I didn't fulfill the criteria of the lovely feminine woman from day one. I was in a constant dis-ease of where I fit in. Fortunately, I grew up in a time when I could crack that open. I got a great education, but it was a great education so I could get a husband.

The first time I understood the beauty of womanhood happened during childbirth. Something elemental takes over your body. It's a thing of great mystery and lusciousness. I had my children at home with a midwife (I had to take a stand on this). Going through that process, nursing my infants and loving many aspects of motherhood absolutely were transformative in my joy of being a woman. I understood what it meant to want to simply nurture my children and saw that as an incredibly important thing to do. Until you have children, you don't know what that is. Giving my time and effort to raising my children wasn't anti-feminist; it wasn't to the detriment of my own fulfillment. The other feelings (about being a woman) didn't go away completely, but I changed that core understanding of what a woman's body is capable of, and knew on a visceral level, the miracle of it and the beauty of it.

Frankly, I didn't like women in general. I loved conversations with men, I loved the action. But after experiencing childbirth, I began to enjoy being a woman.

The alternative men of my generation—my ex was one— would say they were feminists. They were gentle and more willing to express their emotions, but there were certain ways in which they still hung on to the center of power in relationships. There came a point when I had to say to my husband, "I want things to be different and if they're not, I can't stay in the relationship." He couldn't do it. We tried different things and still, it was the same dynamic over and over.

I was finally coming to a place of power; childbirth gave me some of that. Being hippy back-to-the-land homesteaders was fine for a while, but independent of my relationship with him, I began to be recognized as a teacher. I worked with special needs kids. My world was expanding, not just as a woman, but also as someone with skills and a contribution to make, and he stayed back there. He didn't grow.

That was a turning point for me, and the marriage couldn't survive. I couldn't fix it any more. Then it became a question of saving my own life. The kids were still ten and twelve. It was complicated and painful, but I left him. I believed that I had a right to craft a life for myself. And to get positive feedback in the larger world telling me I had something to offer. Shortly after that, I came out as a lesbian.

I believe that there's a spectrum from straight to gay; I hadn't totally claimed that before. I was probably bisexual before I came out. I think we can have the flexibility to find what is most engaging and connecting and erotic at different times in our lives. I didn't have a bad sexual relationship with my husband. But when I met men and dated them, I didn't like the ways in which they related to me and to life; I didn't like what they expected of me as a woman, in terms of taking care of them.

A lot of the men I met weren't self-actualized. They were smart but needy and wanted and needed a fair amount of nurturing. I wanted a reciprocal relationship without hierarchies. I wanted the connection to be face-to-face, genuine, so that we're evolving together— not that we don't take care of each other, but that's not the core of our relationship. The core of it is mutual respect and understanding; that was more important to me.

I dated both men and women after my divorce; then I had a choice to make. Oh, that's who I am. It was another layer of discovery. I met my current partner when I was forty-five. When I was married, lesbianism was never an issue. I had experimented in college, but it was fleeting. As I said, I was always oriented toward men; I liked the company of men. My husband was a contemporary guy. It wasn't that I changed into someone else.

There are actually many gay people in my family, but the ethic in my family was to accept them but not to talk about them, just like we never talked about my mother's drinking. I cracked open the family. I came out in 1992. When I was a kid a lesbian was considered an unattractive woman who couldn't get a man. (Anyway, this is what I internalized as a kid: It was not an option, definitely a secret to keep.) My mother was accepting; she wasn't judgmental about it. She was glad I divorced my ex because she thought he was a deadbeat in terms of earning a living.

Each of these turning points was building on the sense of who I am or who I might be in allowing things to develop. They each created a foundation for me to change in riskier ways: with childbirth—I actually love my woman self; with divorce, I love myself. Lesbianism is about knowing who you are, about self, sexuality, making a complicated choice in terms of culture. This feels real, and it's who I am, and who I'll be for the rest of my life.

The last turning point was my discovery of the wilderness as home. At this point, journey and home have merged. I want to go on long distance hikes, but I also love being home; they aren't in contradiction. That's a continuum too.

We built a simple home up in Carson near Taos, where I go every weekend I can. It's one room, twenty by thirty, with a wood-burning stove. I go up and write. It's a luxury. I split the wood, haul my water, use the outhouse. I need that sense of returning to the land for rural quiet to find what I need to say and write about. This is a place that I created; it feeds me and gives me sustenance.

You can have a thousand voices in your head questioning what you're doing: Why should I give myself permission to write? In New Mexico, you have support to be creative. The landscape gives it to you, because it's always awakening. I can go to that mental and physical space that I created myself and discover that part of myself that I couldn't find when there are too many voices in my head. I have to go up there to rediscover that again and peel away the layers and get to the core.

I found my voice writing about my experiences in the wilderness, which I unabashedly love and have no restraints about. Something cracked open. My writing is immensely better for it. So is my writing voice.

I travel to and write about places that are so beautiful: the embrace of forest, moisture, color, leaves and these trails. Then there's the sense of endlessness and openness, so much to explore. It's just so inspiring and emotionally moving—that's what I began to want to experience more and more.

Then add staying over night from one night to three weeks. To feel that nourishment—the longer you go, you do get exhausted; but the more you go out, the more it becomes a way of being. You pay attention to the scene around you; you shift certain kinds of observations and gain others. That's what I seek. I want to go on longer and longer treks. I yearn to do that: to go for three months or six months.

When you hike in the wilderness, there's no beginning and no end. You're just there. You go through so many eco systems, even in a day walk— down and up, challenging your body, experiencing periods of euphoria where you're sailing along. I'm slow on the incline but it feels great. At the top, you take that deep breath and let your heart settle down and there you are. It's just compelling. That's the beauty of it.

The return to me for my physical effort makes it home too: an invitation, an earthy room defined with bigger, more amorphous boundaries, that feels very familiar even if it's not the same trail or same mountain range. Yes, what it feels is familiar, and that's the definition of home. When I'm in the wilderness, I am home.

Beatrice Nevares

A Passion for Giving

Beatrice Nevares grew up with parents who were very giving people. They lived near the railroad tracks on Romero Street in Santa Fe and when the hobos would get off the train, her parents had pots of hot coffee and hot chocolate and biscuits and cookies waiting for them on their back porch. That scene of the hobos in tattered clothing gulping hot beverages and freshly baked goods was imprinted on her mind and helped shape the course of her life.

Bea's mother was of Italian descent, the first generation born in the states. Bea's father, who worked for the railroad, came from a Hispanic family in Las Cruces. Bea and her brother and three sisters all went to Catholic schools. Although her parents were strict, she remembers her childhood as very happy. They were united as a family: they ate their meals together and attended church together. Bea admired her parents' long marriage (sixty-two years together) and hoped that she, too, would have a long, happy marriage. She felt closer to her father and often confided in him. When he retired, she enjoyed joining him in the mountains where they'd spend the day together while he painted. Her father never sold his artwork; he preferred to give it away.

When Bea was growing up, she'd often come home from school without her coat or jacket. If someone didn't have one, she'd give them hers without a second thought; sometimes she'd bring an old pair of shoes in to school for someone whose shoes were worn out. Her parents didn't ask questions, but they knew what she was up to.

Although Bea and her siblings were encouraged to have careers, Bea was intent on getting married after high school. In fact, she turned down a scholarship to be with her high school sweetheart. Her parents thought she was too young to marry at eighteen but they didn't stop her. In retrospect, Bea has mixed emotions about her decision to forego the scholarship. She thought her marriage would be forever but it lasted only five years. When it was falling apart, she wondered if she had made the wrong decision, but her marriage gave her two wonderful daughters, so in the long run this made it worthwhile for her. During the divorce and in later years, she and her ex-husband were always civil to each other and still consider each other friends today. She had a second marriage to an older man. A son, who is a Catholic priest, was born from this union; he gives her much pride.

While she was raising her family, she noticed certain characteristics in her children that she had experienced herself. They'd bring school friends home for lunch, who looked like they needed a hearty meal, or they'd come home from school and say that "Tommy" doesn't have much. Bea would send an envelope to school with money to help his family out.

When she was pregnant with her first child, she started working for Bell Telephone as a long distance operator. She worked there for twelve years—first fulltime and then part-time—until her divorce and then went into business with another woman to open an exclusive dress shop, because she was always interested in fashion.

After five years of working in the dress shop, she was bored and restless. She began asking herself, "What am I doing here? This is not me." Almost twenty years in the for-profit world left her feeling hollow and unsatisfied, so she had begun volunteering at a homeless shelter and knew deep down, that's where her heart lay.

Dinner with Sister Shirley, the director of the shelter who was leaving town, changed her life and brought her back to her parents' values. The Sister planted the seed that Bea should start her own shelter. After that, Bea was haunted by the idea, and she looked for a space. She found an old, deserted motel and negotiated a deal with the owner to receive eight months' free rent to start her project. It was in that spot that Bea started Bienvenidos Outreach, Inc., to provide food, clothing, medical assistance, guidance and support to the poor and homeless in 1989.

She was the heart and the soul of the organization for years. Not only did she build the shelter from the ground up, she managed every aspect of it. She'd work on grants, call donors, answer requests to speak, and run its programs. She did all this work willingly, but what she really loved most was talking with the poor and the homeless. Something in her came alive during these conversations; she felt like she was making a difference.

Three years ago, the president of the Board of Directors put pressure on her to retire because she was approaching seventy. She was upset at the obvious age-ism when she had no health problems and had been doing her job more than satisfactorily for nineteen years. But she got tired of clashing with him and felt that their philosophies would never mesh; he wanted her to stay behind her desk and she wanted to be "hands-on," mixing with the homeless. So she retired.

Since her retirement she has not stopped giving and doing for the less fortunate. Working out of her home, she connects with organizations for the homeless and the poor. When she first retired, she'd call around to the non-profits every morning to see who had the greatest need. Now she works with one church group in Los Alamos that brings her clothing and food to distribute every other week. She stores them in her garage and then offers them to LifeLink, a social agency that provides supportive housing, and mental health and addiction treatment services.

Bea Nevares grew up seeing her parents help the less fortunate. She followed in their footsteps as a child, but her interest in the less privileged remained in the background for close to twenty years as she focused on coping with two marriages, raising three children and earning a living. At fifty-one years of age, she rediscovered her passion for giving and opened a shelter for the poor and homeless. Since that time, her work with the less fortunate has been a mission, a passion and a spiritual path. It guides her life. "What can I do today to help?" is the first thing she thinks about when she wakes up in the morning and the last thing she thinks about at night. In her own words, Beatrice Nevares, seventy-two, describes her journey and how opening a homeless shelter not only enriched her own life but brought her home to her deepest self. In the process, she changed the lives of hundreds of people whom she touched.

In her own words....

That dinner with Sister Shirley started a process that took me full circle, back to the values of my parents. I grew up giving to the poor and homeless but once I married, I got off on another track. It was a difficult time—going through two divorces and supporting my growing family. I thought I'd enjoy working at an expensive dress shop but I felt so guilty charging such high prices... It just wasn't me.

Sister Shirley knew the real me. "You have a passion for this work," she said. "You have to start a shelter of your own. "I just laughed and said, "Yeah, me? I don't think so." She said, "You have all the expertise, I taught you everything." Even though I dismissed what she said, she had planted the seed. And I couldn't let it go.

The following week I drove all over town trying to find a good location for a shelter that wasn't expensive. I had no idea what I wanted to do; there was something in my heart that guided me.

I found an old motel that had been closed, and I thought maybe this could be turned into something. I saw mice around; it was dirty and rundown. I said to myself, "What are you doing here? Are you out of your mind?" But I could envision it. I knew the owner and got in touch with him and told him what I wanted to do. He said, "You have to be crazy. How will you finance it?" I told him that I knew how to go about fund raising and getting grants. I pleaded with him, "Give me a chance. Let me have it for six or eight months and see what I can do. If it comes up to par, then you can start charging me rent." He agreed and told me, "As of today, it's yours. Do what you feel is right, and we'll talk at the end of eight months." I came home and asked myself, "What on earth did I get myself into?"

The next day, I got on the phone and called the phone company and told them I needed a phone. I waited for the phone man in the dilapidated motel. When he came in, he said, "You want a phone *here*? This place is horrible." He put in the phone line. Then I called the local newspapers and told them who I was and what I wanted to do. They thought it was a good story. I met with their reporters and told them I needed help: I told them I needed a carpenter, a painter, an electrician and an exterminator. One reporter said, "Whoa, lady."

His article came out a few days later and my phone didn't stop ringing. It was overwhelming. I had friends come and help me. We started fixing up the place. By the end of the third month, the place was so nice. I called the owner and asked him to come over; he couldn't believe it was the same place. I had put in no money out of my own pocket; it was all through donations and the generosity of people that I was able to open a shelter.

We walked through the rooms and sectioned off one for women and families, another for men. I went to the phone again and got bedding and food donated. That's how it started. By the end of the first week we had served thirty-six homeless families and individuals. When I left, almost twenty years later, we were serving three hundred food boxes and three hundred lunch bags each week, and about one hundred-fifty individuals visited the clothing room each week to select donated clothes.

At the end of eight months, the owner started charging rent. I was in that location for two years, and then he wanted to sell the building. I didn't know where I was going to go. My ex, who's a lawyer with a huge office, offered to lend me space for a food bank, but not a shelter. I moved there for almost a year and then another place opened up on Luisa Street, and we set up shop there.

I was the executive director of Bienvenidos for nineteen years. I started a lot of programs, helped with school supplies and uniforms, had Thanksgiving dinner for families, toys for the children at Christmas, Easter baskets. I'd run over on the weekends. I was always thinking, what could I do next? When you have the drive and a vision and you love what you're going, it's amazing what can happen; I had a passion for this work and that helped us get bigger and bigger.

I loved my work there, but eventually, it came to an end. Three years ago, the board president said he was leaving within a year and told me I should retire too because of my age. I said, "My age? What does my age have to do with it?" He kept talking about my age, so I made the decision to move on. I found someone to run it, and I hope Bienvenidos survives. If not, I did my best.

I wanted to be hands-on with the homeless. I'd be sitting at my desk, and I'd hear their stories, and they'd be turned away, so I'd get out from behind my desk and call them back. One woman said to me, "Why do you dirty your hands with *those people*?" I said, "What do you mean—*those people*?" She said, "They're dirty and messy, and won't help themselves. " I said, "Maybe so, but if you take the time to listen to them and feed them, you can help them get back on their feet."

I'm a bird that's been set free. Now I can do as much or as little as I want. When I first retired, I'd call the soup kitchen or another nonprofit in the morning and see what kind of help they needed that day. I had offers of jobs, but I want to be free now to do what I want to do. If I see a homeless person on the street, I'll stop and help him. If I want to use my own money to buy a person a pair of shoes or take him out to a fast food restaurant, I can.

I can't complain about anything; I'm happy. I volunteer but I don't want to be on a schedule. I do a lot of freebies on my own. I connected with another lady who works with the homeless and the poor and do referrals for her. She works with LifeLink, another program for women with children and the homeless. I help them out, but I'm behind the scenes now.

I want to let go of the less fortunate, but I can't. I still have my mind and my heart with them. I thought about starting another shelter, but with the economy now, it's probably not the best time. I don't know when I'll ever stop; I love doing what I'm doing. There's a great need here.

What most people don't realize is that even though I'm giving, I've gained so much from the poor and the homeless. At seventy-two years of age, I have a lot of compassion, a lot of forgiveness and a lot of generosity. I've learned not to judge by appearance. Don't look at their clothes. Look into their eyes and see how they're hurting and talk to them about what brought them to this place.

This is my life's work and my true home. I feel like this work is a calling, almost like my son's calling to be a priest. It has brought me closer to my faith and to God; after all, He walked with the poor and the homeless. It's also taken me full circle, back to my childhood home where my parents used to give the hobos free beverages and baked goods on our back porch. I have come home in many ways and it feels good.

Gloria Feldt

Reclaiming Her Voice

Growing up in West Texas in the 1950s, Gloria Feldt knew with certainty that she was loved and cherished, because she was surrounded by adults who adored her. Until the age of nine, she and her parents and younger sister lived in Temple, Texas with her maternal grandmother, Rose Hendler, who was always there, cooking, chatting, hovering. Every day when Gloria came home from school, they'd play Canasta for hours. Her paternal grandparents lived nearby too and they were always in and out of each other's houses. There was always something going on in Gloria's house: people visiting, friends stopping by, soldiers from Fort Hood without local family staying over for holidays.

When Gloria turned nine, her father's western wear business became successful enough for them to build their own home and move out of her grandmother's. She spent less time with her grandmother then but still saw her often. She was an active volunteer in the community, and, as it turned out, served as a role model for Gloria.

Despite feeling very comfortable in her own home, Gloria never felt "normal" living in Stamford, Texas, where her father moved the family in 1955. Her family was Jewish in a Bible Belt area. Her father owned a business while most of her friends' fathers punched time clocks or farmed. Her mother worked in her father's business, and no one else's mother worked outside the home.

Yet, at the time, she didn't realize just how normal she actually was. In 1957, the United States had the highest teen pregnancy rate in its history. Gloria was one of those statistics. She got pregnant at age fifteen. On hearing the news, her mother cried and her father screamed. Her grandmother reassured her that she'd "make something out of" herself. A few months later she married her high school sweetheart and by the time she was twenty, she had three children.

Gloria was forced by the rules of that era to drop out of high school but got her diploma through a correspondence course. She and her husband had moved to Odessa so he could get a job at General Tire and Rubber Co. It was hard for her to be so far from her family, but at the time she felt very grown-up. In retrospect, she feels she was probably in shock or denial.

She didn't have big dreams for herself—girls those days weren't encouraged that way, but she always loved reading, writing and learning new things. After her third child was born, she began taking classes at the community college and soon became involved in the civil rights movement. This led her to volunteer at the new Head Start program, where she was later offered a teaching position. In 1973, the University of Texas opened a campus in Odessa, so she went back to college full time to finish her degree. Soon after, she wrote a paper on voluntary family planning for her last college course in 1974, and that led to her being offered a position as the head of the local Planned Parenthood. She worked there for four years, turning a small, new affiliate into a middle-sized one.

Gloria and her husband grew in different ways. She had continued her education and had created a professional life for herself; he stayed at the same job his entire life. The times were right for her to move on. It was 1975: Thanks to the women's movement, women were using the birth control pill and earning their own living, so they were less reliant on men and had more life options. After eighteen years together, Gloria said, "there was nothing left there," and so they divorced.

A few years after her divorce when her youngest child was soon to graduate from high school, she was itching to get out of West Texas, so she applied for a position to head the Planned Parenthood in Phoenix, Arizona. She got the job and spent eighteen years leading Planned Parenthood of Central and Northern Arizona, growing it from a small affiliate to one of the four or five largest in the country. During her time in Phoenix, she married an insurance executive who had been on Planned Parenthood's board there. Between them, they have six children, ten grandchildren and four great grandchildren.

In 1996, the national organization, Planned Parenthood Federation of America, recruited her to become its President and CEO. She held the position for nine years. During that time, she became the persona and the voice of Planned Parenthood. It was a heady job: walking the corridors of power, bumping elbows with senators, working with rich and famous supporters. She especially enjoyed the chance to revitalize the organization and create a new vision for it and to have a nationwide and even global impact on women's rights and access to reproductive health care. It was a career far beyond her dreams, but midway through her tenure as President, she realized she had sold her soul; she had completely lost her self in the organization. In her own words, Gloria Feldt, sixty-eight, reflects on how she came to this realization and how she has worked to reclaim her true self—find her own voice and speak from her heart—in the last few years.

In her own words....

It's a wonderful thing to turn your life's passion into your life's work. It's also wonderful to have a mission that's bigger than yourself, but the negative side of that is that I was completely consumed by it. After a while, there were no boundaries. I completely lost myself. I don't know exactly when that happened.

I started out thirty years ago in West Texas with a small, new affiliate, and grew it to a much larger one. I learned that I enjoyed growing something; that was very gratifying. Next I took on the Phoenix affiliate. They had adopted a bold strategic plan to open clinics all over their service area. I was naïve enough to believe I could do that, and I did. I stayed in Phoenix for eighteen years and this time, I grew an undersized organization to one of the country's largest. That was the greatest fun.

In the process, the social and political climate was changing. I had to learn how to operate in politics, how to lobby, how to do grass roots organizing. Attacks were growing on reproductive rights, so I had to learn to respond to that. Actually, I had to learn *not* to respond but to set the agenda, but that's another story. With each additional responsibility, I got more consumed and became more of a public persona. I was representing the organization, not me. People related to me as the face and voice of the organization.

I understood that the organization and the mission were what I was about; I wasn't promoting myself. I got pretty good at promoting Planned Parenthood. So good, in fact that in 1996 the national Planned Parenthood recruited me to head their organization. That's when I went from frying pan into the fire. If I thought my life was consumed in Phoenix, it was nothing compared to the national organization. This was national level politics and fund-raising at a huge level. National had to raise its every dime every year. When I started, we raised forty million dollars. Because I took over the organization when it was in difficult financial straits, I had to go into growth mode. The year I left we raised sixty-six million dollars. Oddly enough, the election of a pro-choice president was bad for us: With Clinton in the White House, many who had been active became complacent; they went on to support other causes.

The affiliates spent the Eighties and early Nineties defending what they had won. In fact, the whole political system of the pro-choice movement is built around defending what it won. But I had a different mind set. What I figured out from growing the "courage muscles," so to speak, is to set your own agenda. Be the thermostat and set the temperature. Don't be a thermometer that just measures it. That's the part of politics I like, and that's what I told the Planned Parenthood affiliates when I became the national president. Gaining the courage to do that was a transformational thing for me. For a woman who grew up in West Texas in the Fifties, you don't learn that you have the power to set an agenda. You're taught to react, not be proactive. I learned on the job how to do this.

After a few years in Arizona and well before I took the national position, I woke up one day and thought, what if we had our own legislation? Why not ask for money for family planning? Why not ask for money for prevention? Let's see who will fight us on that. It was a worthy strategy, and I brought this optimistic perspective to the national role. It completely changed the conversation. So I gave people new programs, policy initiatives, and fresh ideas to rally around. I engaged the whole organization and together we created a new twenty-five-year vision that energized the movement. That was great fun. I loved what I was doing, but I took on too much.

My days were all different but generally I spent a quarter of my time on fund-raising, a quarter on politics, a quarter on internal management, a quarter with the affiliates and giving speeches, and another half (or so it seemed) on coalition-building. You can see why I had no time to myself!

I completely let myself be branded by Planned Parenthood. It was like I had a scarlet P on my forehead. I first realized that I had lost myself about half way through my tenure as national president.

Because of my twenty-two years as an affiliate CEO, I had the trust of the affiliates; nevertheless, once the role changes so does the relationship. Being a leader means you have to lead, and not everybody is happy with you all the time. The affiliates I ran had boards made up of local leaders who were supportive and engaged in raising money and using their political influence for us. The national organization, being a federation, had a very difficult governing structure for a CEO to work with. The national board is there to watch you on behalf of the affiliates that are usually engaged in a power struggle to retain control over the money and the policies. Despite these internal politics, I still had to raise all the money for the national organization myself. The national board didn't fund raise as a general rule, and few of them seemed to appreciate the work I was doing to support and expand affiliates. It was the same thing with politics: It was up to me to fashion political relationships at the national level. It was enjoyable, heady to be in the halls of power, but it was lonely, very lonely without that support system I was used to having.

As national president, there were no other organizations in our field of the size and scope of Planned Parenthood. The pressures were heavy. Halfway into my tenure, I had this feeling that if I didn't start writing books, I was going to die. Writing had always captured my heart and soul. I've always loved the writing process; I love putting my hands on the keyboard.

At that point, I realized that there was a way I could put the two—my job and my soul—together. I tried that first. I wrote two books for Planned Parenthood. I thought they would be useful vehicles to get our message out in a sound-bite media world that increasingly polarized the issues. That has proven to be true. People to this day, especially young women, tell me my books influenced them to get involved as an activist, make a career in the field, or to better understand the politics of reproductive rights.

I was concerned that individual stories got lost in the polarized environment. The media wants extremes. What I had learned is that everyone has a story and rarely is it extreme; usually it has shades of gray. These stories were difficult, interesting and inspiring. I had collected hundreds of letters and stories over the years and wove them into a book called *Behind Every Choice is a Story*. Then I wrote the political side of it in a book called *The War on Choice,* which was about all the ways the Bush administration was trying to take away our reproductive rights.

With these books, I thought I could make my talent for writing benefit Planned Parenthood and coincidently feed my soul. Clearly that wasn't enough to please everyone.

I didn't even ask for the copyright in my name. I didn't ask for anything. Those books don't belong to me. That pisses me off. I'm angry with myself that I didn't have the sense to claim those rights. I used every spare moment I had for myself to write them: I wrote evenings, weekends, on my vacation, all the while spending the same sixty plus hours a week on the rest of the job. Why didn't I have enough sense to obtain at least a co-copyright? It all came crashing in, and I had to move on. From an emotional perspective, that's why I left. Thirty years was also a good round number—I had been planning to leave when I reached that point in 2004, but wanted to get us through the 2004 elections first.

When I left, I was so tired. Yet, at the same time, I knew that if I were ever going to write the books that were important to me, I had to write them *now*. That sounded easy but the rest of the world still saw me as the voice and face of Planned Parenthood. I could change how I saw myself more easily than others could change how they saw me. That made it difficult to do some of the things I was interested in doing when I left.

I had an idea for a book that I thought would use the legitimate knowledge I had but would start to move me into another realm. I wanted to write about America's difficult relationship with sex. We talk about sex education but not about sexual pleasure. America's unhealthy relationship with sex is causing so many of the problems we deal with. We have the highest teen pregnancy rate, the highest abortion rate, and on and on. Other countries have a better attitude about sex.

I really wanted to write about *that*, but I couldn't get an agent to take it on. My book agent suggested instead of writing that, I write Kathleen Turner's biography. I knew Kathleen, because she was a volunteer for Planned Parenthood for years. But I felt I didn't know how to write that book, and we were both quite reticent about doing it. Yet Kathleen and I had something in common: we were both at turning points in our careers. She decided it was a good time to look back on what she had learned and share that with other women, so eventually that's what we decided to do.

Publishers weren't interested in a biography, which would have made it *my* book. They were interested in a memoir, which is *her* book. It's her book, her life—very different than writing a biography. My agent told me I'd be advancing women's causes by telling her story. That was true, but at the same time, I made myself invisible again. I was speaking in someone else's voice. I still couldn't speak in my own voice. *I let this happen again.*

In a sense, though, writing Kathleen's book, which is called *Send Yourself Roses: Thoughts on My Life, Love and Leading Roles,* gave me a year to come to terms with my pattern of speaking in someone else's voice. It was like a year's psychotherapy. I lived her life as I was writing it. When you can put yourself into someone else's problems, it helps you solve your own. I realized as a girl growing up, I was socialized to be adaptable, to be a servant, to help others, not to have goals of my own. I was to be the support system, the wife and mother. I *was* encouraged to become educated, but there was always something inside wanting to get out that never quite did or could. Other people look at my life and say, "Oh, my God, you've done these incredible things," and that's true, I appreciate that. Now that I'm on the other side of the process, I value what I did even more.

Nonetheless, I felt powerless. I never used my own voice, my own persona. I'm still working on that: My commitment to myself and to other women is to embrace my own power *with intention*. This is what I feel I have to offer. I was never intentional until now. I decided I'd write a book about women's relationship with power, how women avoid power, and why now is our moment to claim it.

This *is* an incredible moment: we have to do it now. We've made a sea change in gender equality. The trend of women being over half of college students, half of law and med students is incredible. But women are still only 17% of Congress, 15% of corporate boards. We're educating ourselves and the doors are open; there are no legal barriers. It's in our hands to walk through the doors with intention. The historical pattern, however, is that we walk up to the door and then stop ourselves. My legacy is to share what I've learned in hopes that younger women will start earlier than I did and think about their lives with more intention. When I speak today at universities, young women tell me that the March for Women's Lives in April 2004 was the event that got them radicalized or activized. That's great!

I feel good now that I'm doing the things I love best: writing and speaking. I learned to become a pretty good CEO (I joke that I had to be a CEO because I can't type!), and I did the job well, but if I look back on my life, that's probably not what I would have done if I had lived *my* life with intention. If I had done *that*, I would have probably become a writer. From the time I was five years old, I carried around a notebook and wrote poems. I was a published author at four! I wrote stories all the time, but then I became a teenager and my hormones kicked in.

I was a smart little girl but not that physically active. I went to the public library every week. I'd borrow the library cards of my mother and both of my grandmothers, so I could take out sixteen books a week! I always loved words: Writing them or reading them or listening to them. Being an only child for five and half years until my sister was born, I always had a lot of alone time and I liked it; I've always been comfortable with quiet. Oddly, I came to love the public fray—what an adrenaline rush! Now I crave the alone time. I'm learning to trust my own mind and my own judgment; I don't have to consult with the whole world. I'm recognizing my own power to do things my own way. Part of that comes with age; you become more comfortable in your own skin. You just flat out don't care about some things.

After I quit my job, it took me a few months to phase out. I had to go through papers at Planned Parenthood and finish up things. At the same time, I was so tired. I needed to sleep for a couple of months and not do anything different. Then I floundered. I wanted to write, and I enjoyed speaking. I didn't want another regular job again. I was sixty-three, not old enough to retire but old enough to want to shift. My husband had given up his career in Arizona to move to New York with me when I became Planned Parenthood's president. He put up with my being on the road constantly for nine years. I wanted to be at home now. I felt like I owed it to him to be present.

Step by step, I went through a process of getting greater and greater clarity. I saw myself going back to my feminist roots. Also, I didn't have to be nonpartisan any more, I could say what I wanted to say, and I didn't have to compromise politically. That was so liberating!

Originally, I got into reproductive rights through civil rights and the women's movement. For me it was always a feminist issue. I could wear my Republican pearls when I had to, but at heart I'm about women from a very feminist perspective. It was like peeling off these layers and getting back to my own core—little by little. After I left my job, I got my ears pierced so I could wear those beautiful dangly earrings. This sounds like a small thing but believe me, this was a big deal at the time—a total departure from my lifelong opposition to piercings of any sort, as the result of which I had always worn those buttoned-up little clip earrings that fit close to the ear. No more. Dangly earrings for me all the way—flowing and free.

The first time I was referred to as a feminist author rather as former president of Planned Parenthood, I almost celebrated. I was giving a speech in a university setting. I felt like I was starting to get my own identity back.

It's an excellent thing to make a big change at this stage of life. I hadn't anticipated that. Being in my early sixties, it's wasn't too late to do something new. Actually how lucky am I to do something new! It gives you a whole new energy. As Kathleen Turner told me, "Never repeat your successes." Do something new and different each time.

My book on women and power, entitled *9 Ways Women Can Change How We Think About Power,* will be released in October 2010. It's advice I wish someone had given me, and I hope it will help other women. When I'm not working on the book, I write op-eds or commentary and I have my own website blog. I still make speeches and I serve on the board of the Women's Media Center. I discovered social media: Facebook, Twitter. There is something that draws me to it. Actually I'm attempting to wean myself from spending so much time there, but I have met some really fabulous people that way. It's become my water cooler. I was always in an office with a lot of people or at meetings or speaking to others. Most days I'm alone working now. When I get bored or tired or stuck, I flip over to Facebook for a minute and then come back to my writing.

When I left my thirty-year career with Planned Parenthood that had culminated with being the national president and CEO for nine years, I was like a bowl of jelly. Without the organizational structure and the external political pressures that had defined my life for so long, I felt adrift, and it has taken me some time to get to know my true self. Of course, it was there all along, but I had subsumed it to the larger mission of the movement.

I'm slowly getting there. There hasn't been one defining moment. For myself, the separation has been a little bit at a time. I will always have the passion in my heart for the issues, but it's hard to separate from an organization that's a brand name. Leaving Planned Parenthood was almost like experiencing a death. I went through all the stages and it took a year. At the one-year mark, I felt differently: I wasn't as obsessed about what was happening there and now I don't care at all. People tell me I look ten years younger. And I'm actually sleeping—not getting four hours of sleep and rising at the crack of dawn to make three speeches in one day while subsisting on airport food.

I'm still a work in process, but I'm calmer and feeling more integrated. I'm not working less, but I'm enjoying it more. I'm still fairly driven, and I'd say I'm slightly obsessed with writing all the books on the list I made for myself after leaving Planned Parenthood. I'm appreciative of the good health that allows me to feel I have at least another twenty years to do them. But the difference is that now I'm writing them for *me* in *my* voice and those copyrights will be in my name!

Patricia Joseph Lewis

Coming Full Circle

Coming Home

As a little girl living in Toledo, Ohio, Patty Joseph followed her mother around the house and learned all the domestic chores necessary to maintain a traditional Middle Eastern home. Her parents, who were first generation Lebanese, retained many of the customs of the old country. Holidays were elaborate affairs celebrated with the extended family. The women cooked for days making stuffed zucchini, meat pies, and a whole stuffed lamb or *kibbi,* which always had the imprint of the cross on it to bless it. They set the table with the best linens. Patty loved helping her mother and grandmother in the kitchen and was also responsible for doing all the ironing for her parents and three brothers.

Growing up, Patty wanted to be just like her mother, who never worked outside the home and didn't learn to drive until she was in her thirties. Her father, who was in business with his three brothers and their father, quit high school to run their butcher shop. Over the years, they expanded into supermarkets and then delved into real estate. As part of the traditional culture, Patty was expected to live at home until she married and follow their rules while she lived under their roof.

As she became a teenager, though, Patty couldn't wait to try her wings. She felt constrained by all the family rules and restricted by their old-world customs. She yearned to express herself in a more modern way. She defied her father, who wanted her to go to college locally so she could live at home, and her mother, who wanted her to go to an all girls' school. Instead she went to Ohio University, a big party school. Free at last, she felt like a bird sprung from its cage.

After graduation, her mother asked her to come home for a year. She did, and regretted it from day one. Living under her parents' roof, she had to follow their curfews and other rules once again. Patty eventually moved to Cleveland, feeling as though she had broken her father's and her grandfather's hearts. They both died while she was there, and she regrets to this day that she didn't receive their forgiveness for leaving home.

After a year or two in Cleveland, she moved to New York City, where she worked for a nonprofit for ten years. Then, realizing she needed to make more serious money, she started taking economics and business classes hoping to break into the brokerage business. It was a long shot, considering her background, but she eventually landed a job at Merrill Lynch and later transferred to Drexel Burnham. "I'm a great asset gatherer," she told me. "I give off something that allows people to open up to me and trust me. Maybe it's my social work mentality." Successful beyond her dreams, at one point, she had eighty-five million dollars under her management.

Work became her entire life. She rarely dated, had no hobbies, never read a book or cooked a meal any more. Her refrigerator held a container of yogurt and three kinds of cheese: Cheddar, Jarlsberg and Camembert. She frequently stopped for Chinese food on her way home from work. Then, she'd collapsed into bed as the ten o'clock news filled the empty air in her thirty-second floor apartment.

She loved her clients and hearing their stories and helping them. But after two decades, she was bone tired. She knew it was time to call it quits. She began meditating to give her some clarity about her life. As she acknowledged that she needed more balance, she consciously worked to find a man. She attended every social function she could, even if it meant taking time away from work. She stopped working twenty-five years to the day she entered the business, found and married her soul mate at age fifty, and moved to the southwest in 2005.

Over the last five years she has become known as the Mayor of Coyote (the name of her street). She gives fabulous dinner parties, renown for her cooking and the careful, elegant way she sets her table, often matching her table settings to the season or the holiday. As she places platters on the buffet table, guests will often hear her talk about how her mother or grandmother prepared certain foods. In one way, she may have traveled far from her roots, but in another, she has come full circle, bringing the Middle Eastern traditions of home-focused, gracious entertaining that she grew up with into her new home as a sixty-five-year-old Lebanese woman married to a Jewish widower.

Patty's coming home, however, has expanded and deepened beyond the walls of her kitchen. She has also discovered a creative side she never knew she had: She took classes to learn watercolor painting and found she loved painting scenes from nature. For several years she painted on her kitchen counter and then turned a storage room into a home studio to support her newfound talent. If Patty is not in the kitchen cooking or in her studio painting, you'll find her curled up with a good book, another interest she developed recently. In the following section, Patty Lewis reflects, in her own words, on her interesting journey, which brought her home to her deepest self.

In her own words....

The traditions of the old country were very much alive in my family. Boys and girls have certain roles, and boys are definitely more valued. The families stick together and settle in clusters, whether it's in Cedar Rapids, Iowa or Detroit, Michigan. They want that camaraderie, and most are Eastern Orthodox. There were two churches in our town, and my dad was in the family business—it was exactly like *Avalon*, the movie.

I had a strong relationship with my grandmother. But there's such control in the Middle Eastern culture: I remember we were making these little Syrian breads. I patted mine and thought it was done. Then she moved my hand aside and patted the bread for the last time. She had to have the last pat! I made an apple pie years ago and my grandmother told my mother it was as good as hers. Mother resented it. I never made another apple pie.

Holidays we were always together, with traditional Middle Eastern foods at my grandparents' house. My mother didn't work; she stayed at home and ran the household and orchestrated everything. She married at seventeen and had four kids fairly soon. It was probably very overwhelming for her as a young woman.

I always had household chores even though we had help. The bad news is I got stuck with the ironing. It was a bone of contention in the end. For years, after I left home, I never ironed. Now ironically, I love to iron again *because it's my choice.*

I was one of three girls out of seventeen grandchildren. My grandfather and father never forgave me for leaving home before I married. I could leave for college; that was okay but after that, I should live at home. I moved away and they both died while I was gone. I felt like I had killed them. I thought I'd never get over it. My brothers never left and they referred to me as the smart one, the one who got away.

Even though my mother was upset that I left home, she did come to New York and help me look for an apartment. She charmed the landlord into giving us a good deal, but I still couldn't make the rent, so she helped me for several years. I was surprised that she did that, but I think she saw in me what she didn't have in herself: the gumption to make it in the world.

When I got to New York I was pretty broken. I ended up living in Brooklyn with an airline stewardess and had my first big love affair. I was petrified all the time, especially of the subway. I'd take a cab to Brooklyn! Somehow I survived. I got a job at United Cerebral Palsy for eighty-five-hundred dollars a year where I worked as a teacher of the deaf, then I became assistant director, and then director. I stayed for ten years. It was an amazing place to work with physically handicapped adults.

After I had been at United Cerebral Palsy for about eight years, I realized I wasn't an heiress and had to get a job for real money. It took me two years to do this. The cosmetic industry wouldn't hire me, because I wasn't attractive enough by their standards, and my hair was too thin! I interviewed with several brokerage houses, but they didn't want someone from a nonprofit because you're not profit-oriented. But there was a manager at Merrill Lynch who really was interested in me but didn't think I'd make the cut. I went though their simulation test and failed.

I don't know how I got the gumption to do this, but I said to him, "Listen, I have an idea. I never take vacations. Why don't I take a month off from my job? I'll work for you for nothing with no obligation." No one had ever made such an offer. He agreed to do it. I went to work for him for the month of October and he hired me after seven days.

Thank God the training period was four months. I needed it! There was a stack of books I had to read. I had to take the Securities and Exchange Commission exam, which was six hours long and it dealt with ethics, compliance, and margins. It was not easy but I passed it and went to work for them.

We were expected to make cold calls, and I couldn't do that. I was too frightened. I had taken some motivational sales seminars to get psyched, so every morning I'd wake up and as soon as I put my feet on the floor, I'd chant, "I can do it, I can do it." I chanted until I walked out the door to go to work at seven a.m. At the office, you go through a ritual: you have to read the research, see what happened the day before. You line up who you'll call, what you'll sell, what bonds were available. You eat lunch at your desk and stay on the phone all day. You don't put the phone back on the cradle. One month I had one hundred-eighty-five dollars worth of charges on my credit card for Chinese food. I stopped cooking and cleaning the apartment. I did very well very quickly. By the end of my second year I was doing what most people do after five years.

Cash management accounts were just beginning. I did well at gathering assets. You tell me of all your assets, and I'll comment on them and you'll probably bring them to me. I was able to bring in large sums of money from people because they trusted me. That was the biggest key to my success: the relationships I built. I liked listening to people's stories and injecting my opinion. I'd visit these old people living on Fifth Avenue. One woman had thousands of shares of Pfizer stock. I tried to convince her to diversify, but she never did. I probably wasted a lot of time visiting these people in their homes, but that was what I found fascinating about the business.

Toward the end of my work life, I started meditating. I realized I needed to get in touch with myself and figure out what I wanted to do with the rest of my life. The spiritual side of life always intrigued me, but I never had time to pursue it. I went to a seminar on Transcendental Meditation and received a mantra. Once I started meditating at home, I was totally blown away by the changes I experienced. I saw the difference so quickly. When the market crashes, everything is in chaos. But when you meditate, things just come at you a lot slower; nothing gets blown out of proportion. When I was meditating, watching the screen was not so chaotic. Meditation slowed my reactions down and slowed down what came at me. I could hear people better, I calmed down in terms of getting upset about things. There were pretty profound differences. I meditated two times a day for four years.

And I did work hard to meet a man. I got out there a lot. I went to parties, singles forums. I even used a dating service. I ended up meeting Bob at a party given by a client of mine; he was her cousin. When we started going together, I had to juggle work and my life with him. That was intense. We married, lived apart for a year, and then lived together.

I was in the business (at different firms) twenty-five years to the day. I started on January 2, 1980 and retired on January 2, 2005. In those twenty-five years, I had great retention of my business. But by the end, I was so tired. I had met Bob, and we wanted to do something different with our lives. But I didn't see how I could leave these people in the middle of a bad market (2000). I worked out an arrangement where I was working part-time with two business partners, so I wouldn't let my clients down. My partners eventually won the trust of my clients and took over my business.

We moved out west in May 2004. I officially ended my work the following January. I wanted to come to the southwest, but when we got here, I found it dry, dusty, sandy, and windy; it made me crazy. I thought I had made a mistake. At the same time, buying this house felt right even though it was an impulsive decision. But all that dust, and then a pit bull jumped over the fence and scared me. The howling of the coyotes drove me crazy.

For my sixtieth birthday, my friends came from all over the country to help me celebrate. There was a full rainbow at daybreak; I knew it was meant to be. After that, things just started to turn around. As the houses built up in this neighborhood, I kept inviting people over. This is the most amazing community. I just felt I was in the right place to entertain and welcome others. I wasn't running in a hundred directions. It's my caretaking. I had new people to dinner, introduced them to other people. Leaving work was very hard for me; I was used to having people need me. My entertaining filled that need.

When we first got here, I had nothing to do. Are we going to have tea at ten o'clock in the morning? It was overwhelming. I had no hobbies. My life had been 100% work. In the beginning, I did go to the gym, which I hate, and Bob loves. We did some hiking, but I can't take the heat so don't like to hike in the summer. I read *The Year of Magical Thinking* and decided to start a book club. There are now nine of us. It was a good way to get things going socially, but I hadn't read a book for twenty-five years. Reading was monumental for me! I picked brainless books at first, because I'm a slow reader. After I had been reading for a while, though, my speed got better, and I felt I could read more books in a month; sometimes I'd have two books going at once. I felt like I missed a whole section of the world because I never read.

I've always wanted to paint. I signed up for watercolor classes at the community college and took them three times. The fourth time, I took lessons privately. I just love it! I find it very meditative when you get in a zone. At this point, though, I'm not sure where I'm going with this. I have to figure out if what I'm doing truly pleases me. I also feel that I need to learn the basics of drawing, perspective, moving into the distance, and so on. I'm getting better, but I'm still not where I want to be. My painting is loose and fluid, kind of spiritual. I'll go with it and see what it's like. Now that I have my own tiny studio, that feels affirming.

At age sixty-five, I'm discovering who I am and coming home to who I thought I was. I have a lot of involved dinner parties. Being raised in a Middle Eastern family, there was all this elaborateness around dinner parties. I couldn't do that while I was working but now, I'm so comfortable with it. I have fun at my own parties, and everyone loves to congregate at our house. They like to see how I set the table, what I serve. When I have a dinner party I always serve buffet style. I don't like to put food on people's plates.

That's who I was all along, but I didn't get a chance to be it. I was always sidetracked, mostly by my career. When I was working, I got a high off it. But underneath my busyness, I had a lot of anxiety about being alone. I worked on the forty-eighth floor and lived on the thirty-second floor and never felt grounded. One day I took myself to the movies because it was on the ground floor! I loved my work but was terrified that I'd be alone in life. Once I realized I *could* make it if I were single, that changed everything. Then I started to meditate; it relaxed me enough to meet Bob.

Things are different now. Not too much rattles me anymore. I have arrived at a place where I always wanted to be; this is the vision I had for myself. In 1984, I wrote a visualization of what I wanted my life to be. I was in the security business at the time. I visualized that the man I would meet would be a bald professor. (Bob is.) In my home life and in my work life, I'd make people feel comfortable and confident. I brought this visualization to fruition. I used to have a lot of dinner parties in my small studio apartment before I was in the security business, but then I lost all that when I threw myself into my work.

I used to read a lot of books on positive thinking and how to change yourself. One that had a great influence on me was a book called *How People Change by* Allen Wheelis. The message in the book, which I practiced as a way of life, was that the way people change is they practice being what they want to be until they are it. This concept allowed me to create monumental changes in my life. I wrote a visualization, because I needed to create for myself that vision of what I wanted to be and how I wanted to live. This got me to where

I wanted to go, included leaving Toledo, being more than successful in the business world, and creating the personal life I have today. A truly amazing journey that has filled me with great joy!

I am now living the vision I had of home, in every sense of the word. I wish that my mom could share my joy in that; it's too bad for her. Even though I have issues with her, I wish she had been able to come here and see my life, but she resents that I moved so far away. Yet she's still a part of who I am today. If you're at one of my dinner parties, you'll hear me say, "my mother this..." or "my grandmother that..." I bring them into the fold a lot.

I feel like I've arrived in my life. This is where I'm supposed to be. I love my life. My stepdaughters are lovely women. I'm happy to be with a man like Bob, and we have a chance to do what we want to do. The only undercurrent for me is my sadness that my family can't see my life today and that they can't live their own lives to the fullest.

I used to be a person who lived a stressed and exhausted life. I did everything too hard, ran in a lot of directions and was not grounded at all. I regretted the lack of time for reflection and creativity, but for years, I did nothing to change it.

Today I have arrived at the place that I have always wanted for myself: I have the mental and physical space for peace and contentment. It's a place where I don't just come to find these things, but I have the peace of mind to *create* them. Here is where I find my solitude and my own creativity, and where I gather people together so we can all share what we have to offer each other. It's an amazing, magical feeling.

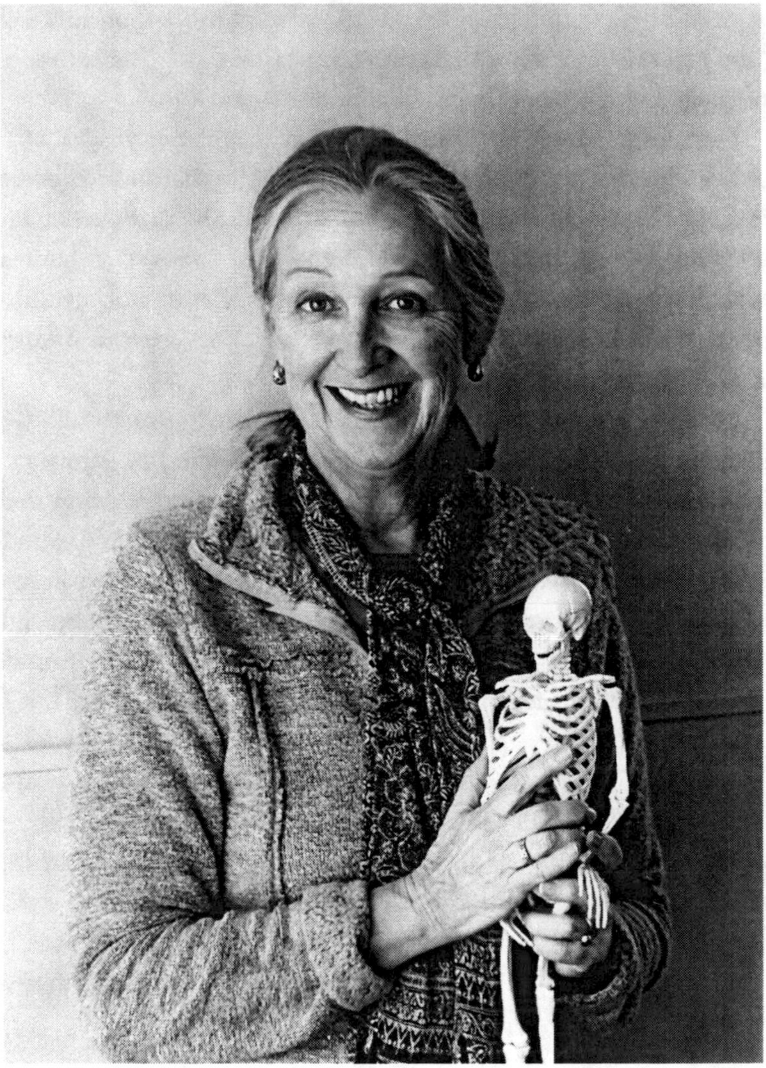

Kathleen Porter

Aligned Body, Mind and Spirit

Coming Home

Before Kathleen Porter was six years old, she lived in a dazzling array of cities—London, Paris, Athens—places where her diplomat father was assigned by the U.S. State Department. Living in ambassadors' residences, surrounded by servants, nannies and chauffeurs, Kathleen's life started out as one of privilege and comfort, yet it was not a happy childhood. Her father was a kind man but formal and distant. Her mother, a former prom queen and debating champion who grew up above a shoe store in Kenosha, Wisconsin lived in her husband's shadow, experienced wide-ranging mood swings, and struggled with alcoholism for decades.

When Kathleen was in grade school, her family settled in Chevy Chase, Maryland, where she grew up with three brothers. For reasons she has never fully understood, she and her siblings grew up as strangers—seldom playing together—and for most of her childhood, she felt very much alone. She was angry with her mother a lot of the time and missed her father's presence, as things tended to be calmer when he was home.

In high school, she didn't feel particularly attractive or smart. Her low self-esteem made her vulnerable to drugs and destructive relationships. She attended the University of Maryland but right before graduation, she dropped out and moved to San Francisco to become a hippie. She regretted not finishing college for the rest of her life.

Although Kathleen yearned to feel close to her parents, she never did until years later. Her mother joined Alcoholics Anonymous after Kathleen left for college, and they never talked about her growing up years. Kathleen felt she never received the unconditional love and acceptance she wanted from her mother, but in later years, she learned of her mother's private struggles with cancer.

After having her thyroid gland removed, her mother underwent a routine hysterectomy at a time when there was no hormone therapy or emotional support for women going through this. Kathleen came to believe these events contributed to her mother's emotional difficulties. As her mother approached death, suffering from dementia, Kathleen realized she was able to give *her* what she had so desperately wanted herself. Giving love, acceptance and forgiveness to her mother brought resolution and healing to the relationship.

In her early twenties, Kathleen began to experience chronic pain: tight shoulders, headaches, and aching jaw. On several occasions, she threw her back out and had to remain bedridden for days. At first she found relief in aerobic exercise and yoga, but it wasn't until she learned about natural skeletal alignment that she found lasting relief.[1]

Growing up near Washington, D.C. Kathleen lived in a world of politics. As early as high school, she became involved in the civil rights movement, and in San Francisco in the late Sixties and early Seventies, she marched against the Vietnam War and went door to door getting signatures for a petition against the war in Cambodia. Knocking on doors in the apartment building in which she lived, she met her future husband, a Chinese-American man from Hawaii. She was attracted to his fun-loving charm and kind nature. He had recently graduated from law school but had "dropped out" and was working as a musician. Together they decided to buy a camper and travel throughout the U.S.

Their adventure on wheels led to marriage and, after settling in Hawaii, three children. Kathleen trained as a massage therapist and became certified to teach yoga, which she did for fifteen years. She later operated a yoga center/bed and breakfast. Her husband had since returned to the practice of law.

After her mother died, her father traveled to Hawaii, at the age of ninety-four, and stayed with Kathleen and her children for a month. Each day she'd take him for a drive, cook his favorite meals, and sit on the side of his bed at night, tucking him in and "talking story." She

---

1 Natural alignment refers to the position of skeletal bones in relationship to each other as intended by the human biomechanical design. Various methods and techniques have been developed in recent years to help people learn how to return to this natural way of inhabiting their body.

was able to say what she'd always wanted to and ask questions about his life. This was one of the most gratifying times in her life. Soon after he returned home, he had a massive stroke and died.

Looking back on her life, Kathleen realized that her desire for a family had caused her to ignore the importance of shared interests and a willingness to communicate in choosing a mate. After twenty-five years of marriage and many years of struggling within the relationship, Kathleen filed for divorce. When her youngest left to go to college, she took a leap of faith and sold the family home and left Hawaii, too.

Without a physical home, she turned inward to try to discover that sense of security and comfort in herself. She had learned about skeletal alignment some years earlier and as she began aligning her own bones in this instinctive way, she became pain-free for the first time in years. Always curious about people who aged well, she took part of the money she made from the sale of her house and used it for a yearlong journey around the world. She traveled to the Cook Islands, Indonesia, Thailand, Vietnam, and Portugal in search of people who have never lost their own natural alignment. On her travels, she spent two months in silent meditation at a forest monastery in Burma.

When she returned to the states in 2004, Kathleen wrote *Ageless Spine, Lasting Health: The Open Secret of Pain-free Living and Comfortable Aging*, and opened The Center for Natural Alignment in Portland, Oregon as a place of self-healing, where people can learn how to reclaim their original structural integrity and return to pain-free living.

Combining her earlier studies of yoga, Alexander Technique, Integrative Yoga Therapy and other somatic techniques with her training and background in massage therapy, Kathleen has spent years studying how the healthy body is designed to be inhabited with comfort and ease. She has taught Natural Alignment through the University of Hawaii in Hilo, the National College of Natural Medicine in Portland, the New Mexico Academy of Healing Arts in Santa Fe, and is currently on the faculty of the Omega Institute in Rhinebeck, New York.

Today at sixty-three, Kathleen Porter's physical home is a room she rents in a friend's house; she has sold or given away most of her possessions.

As she explains in her own words, she has found it freeing to no longer be constrained by the responsibilities and burdens of others' expectations of what a home is supposed to be or by her own expectations of how to compose a life. After years of struggling, Kathleen Porter has come home: not to a building filled with material possessions but to a strong, contented connection to herself and her body.

In her own words....

After having had a large family home with a husband, three children and lots of the usual stuff—furniture, books, toys, uncountable gadgets and a big garden—home at this stage in my life is much more defined by the bond I have with myself, no matter where I happen to be. Because I have cut my ties with an actual physical home, right now I hang my clothes, cook my meals, and sleep at night in one room. Previous to this, I lived almost forty years in Hawaii.

I would never have imagined any of this a few years ago. At that time, I required a home that gave me a sense of assurance and security, as well as an identity as a homeowner and the self-concept of a responsible member of society that came with that. I had very set ideas of what home was supposed to be, decorated a certain way with my personal things and my favorite art. I'm surprised to realize that I don't miss any of that.

I do miss having a place where I can host more than one of my visiting children at a time, but just a few days ago, an old friend who now lives here asked if I would stay with her dog while she travels for three weeks during the holidays. Since telling my children about this, I have discovered all three of them will be coming to spend the holidays with me. I'd say right now it seems that the universe provides!

In spite of the lengthy struggle of up-and-down emotions and dramatic life-changing events that led to changing how I feel about "home," I have to say that now that I've come out the other end of this, I feel very liberated.

I feel that I have arrived at a sense of acceptance and appreciation for myself that I never had before. I have a confidence in both myself and in a somewhat amorphous general underlying goodness that makes life so much more pleasant and enjoyable than it once was. I am able to witness myself often, as if outside myself, moving through the world in a state of wonder at the beauty of not just the natural world, which is so astounding, but the beauty of many little unexpected treasures along the way. Just yesterday I took a friend's dog for a walk to a park with a big pond. There were hundreds of ducks of many varieties, and just as many Canada geese. It was very cold and the sky was gray and dark; the harsh beauty of this scene struck me.

I am able to trust more now. Trust in what, I'm not quite sure, but it has something to do with an overall acceptance of the way things are, and that whatever is happening is ultimately okay, not by any measuring stick, but simply because it is. I live with a greater sense of connection to the world, yet, oddly removed, and not so caught up in trying to analyze or understand it as I once was.

I didn't always have this wisdom. In the past, I tended to be very critical of others and myself. I wasn't very peaceful, feeling somewhat on guard with other people, afraid they would see through me and discover that I was far from perfect. My mind was very active analyzing what was going on in relationships and worrying about possible catastrophes. I had a lot of expectations about the way life was supposed to be. I often gave in to feelings of being inadequate, unattractive and not as smart or good as everyone else. I combated these feelings with a need to present a particular image of myself and to be in control of events and the people around me.

I took things much more personally. I had a very hard time hearing criticism. I cried when I got angry, and I got angry much more often. I was more defensive and less able to see the bigger picture. I was certainly more narcissistic and had trouble putting myself in someone else's shoes, especially if they held a different point of view. I had a history of "upsets" and hurt feelings in various relationships that I would then try to heal by talking them to death. I could never have admitted to any of this at the time, as I was constantly trying to convince myself of how "together" I was.

I don't think there was one particular turning point, but just a gathering of many events, big and small, that contributed to my becoming unstuck. I was stuck in the sense that I was too self-absorbed, too eager to control my environment (and thus, those in it), and never felt quite safe to just be fully relaxed and comfortable in my own skin. Getting unstuck meant a gradual whittling away of my attachment to people, things, and circumstances being the way *I* wanted them to be.

The falling away of these tendencies came in stages over a number of years, first as I became divorced (of my own choosing and, thus, all the guilt and self-recrimination that came with that) and later as I watched my children leave home to go far away to college. I faced an identity crisis when my youngest child left home, and I realized that I didn't know how to live in the world as a single person with no one to take care of, and no one to take care of me.

Because of the range in age of my children (Today they are 33, 27 and 24) and length of my marriage, it had been thirty-two years that I always had someone for whom I was responsible (or at least, believed I was). I had given parenting my all. With my identity so tied up with my children, I struggled to let go of them when the time came for them to leave. Not surprisingly, they didn't always appreciate my hovering attempts to stay deeply planted in their emerging, independent lives. Sometimes they resented me trying to use them as a lifeline. At the same time, I came to the realization that I hated the thought of running a bed and breakfast/wellness center forever and decided to change the channel my life was stuck on. Instead of being left behind in an empty nest I didn't want, I sold the family home and flew out of the nest along with my children. I did this very reluctantly and didn't know at the time what a glorious experience this would actually turn out to be for me.

Years before, I had been introduced to the concept of natural skeletal alignment that was clearly at odds with the way I had been trained to teach yoga. This alignment along the vertical axis of gravity is particular to our species and is what every healthy baby in the world must discover in order to be able to stand and walk. It is also the secret of those small women all over the world who successfully carry heavy loads on their heads with ease. As time went by, there was no denying that aligning my *own* bones in this natural way brought relief from long-standing tensions and chronic pain.

Fascinated by men and women who age gracefully, I decided to travel to places in the world where such people can be found in abundance. As part of my travels, I sat in silent meditation for two months in Burma. I had been a long-time student of meditation but was still ill-prepared for the rigors of this experience. We meditated almost continuously from forty-thirty a.m. until nine p.m. seven days a week. No eye contact. No talk. You had to go into a place in yourself that was unavoidable. You either left or you just kept going. I cried and cried and cried. The front of my blouse would be wet. Day after day I kept going over all the mistakes I'd made over my whole life. I'd go to my interview with the monk and say, "There's so much pain and guilt and sorrow," and he'd say, "Such is the way of the *dharma*," which I took to mean, "You made your bed . . ."

As I sat, I had plenty of time to put principles of alignment into practice as well as reflect on the mistaken beliefs that had been guiding my life. I came face to face with the many false notions I had about myself and others and confronted my insecurities and fears, which had caused me to feel separate from other people for much of my life. I've always had tendencies towards being a perfectionist (that could be hard to believe in some instances). I also had beliefs about the way other people *should be* and had difficulty accepting them when they were not as I expected. People were supposed to be kind, honest, generous or whatever, and the world is supposed to be a just, caring place. I often made myself miserable wanting things to be that way. Through the process of meditation, this broke down. The first month was hell; the second month was a bit more heavenly.

Gradually, I was able to see how much things had changed after those two months. I came to see myself as part of, not apart from, the world in which I live. I started to forgive myself, seeing that I am simply human, like everyone else. I began to release myself from much of the emotional pain and fear that had held me back for so long. I left the monastery a very different person. That sense of feeling a part of the world has never left me for long, although, of course, I still have moments when I feel disconnected, but they tend to be fleeting now.

When I went to the monastery, I didn't have a sense of what home was; I had just sold my home. I didn't have a sense of belonging to the land. For the first time in my life I was "homeless." That process of traveling for a year helped me feel at home *with me*. No matter where I am, home is really wherever I am. I feel safe with myself now. I feel a sense of connection with myself, and feel more at home with others.

Today, I am greatly changed in the way I live and the way I think. My most prized possessions are selected photographs of my family, particularly of my children at various stages of their lives, letters between my parents, and a few favorite books. My other possessions are all functional. Renting a room, I live a bit of the life of a vagabond. I have willingly chosen to put my interest in writing and teaching about natural skeletal alignment before financial security. Being out on the edge financially, especially as I have been writing a second book, has been the trickiest part of the life I now live, but I do manage to keep going.

At a previous time, I often experienced envy, seeing things or circumstances that others had and wishing I could have the same. It's fascinating that I no longer have these feelings *at all*. I'm really content with what I have, and yet I must add the disclaimer that I am determined to earn enough in the near future to assure that I am secure and that I will never be the proverbial "burden" to my children. I'm not there yet, but I'm doggedly working to bring this about.

I find that it's not that hard to live on faith, not faith in any particular belief or dogma, but in something amorphous that I can only sense but would have difficulty describing. At one time, I believed I could only be happy if I were in a relationship with a man, but I no longer believe that to be true, either. It could be lovely in many ways, but it would have to be a really good fit for me to even consider giving up what I've gained for myself.

I live away from my children now, not because I want to, but because they live in places that are limiting to me in terms of what

I want to accomplish at this point. Rather than running off to visit them, I am delighted at how often they show up to visit me. I am blessed to have lovely friendships with mostly women and a few men. These friends have sustained me through the years with a steady stream of love, support and encouragement. Some are new, and some are almost as old as I am. Things are not perfect, and yet they are, of course. Daily life still comes with its challenges. But I am so different in the way I respond and connect with the world now, as well as the way I connect with myself—with acceptance and an underlying joy and satisfaction that feels like it is really here to stay.

I am now truly comfortable in my own skin almost all the time. That's how the principles of skeletal alignment have changed my life and my relationship with my body. With bones aligned to support me, muscles that were storehouses of tension and had to struggle to hold me up or hold me together are now able to relax and be naturally elastic, not too contracted or too slack. The metaphors for how we inhabit our bodies and how this matches how we live our lives are unending. The relaxation of my mind is reflected in the relaxation in my body.

For anyone on a spiritual path, this information brings the body on board as an equal one-third of the body/mind/spirit triad. Beyond the beneficial and complementary practices of meditation and yoga *asana*, aligning our bones is an invitation to be continuously mindful. This approach is not restricted to "the mat" but serves to tie us to the present moment, while sitting, standing, walking, and bending—all elements of working at a computer, getting up to answer the doorbell, bending over to feed the cat, walking to the store or practicing yoga—even lying down to sleep.

If I'm having a conversation with someone, and I'm feeling a growing need to press my point of view or even "be right" about something, I can usually observe my sternum beginning to rise, my chin lifting and my shoulders pulling back. It's as if I can actually feel the ego at work through my body, lifting a protective shield up and creating a physical separation between myself and "the other."

When I am able to have the presence of mind to notice this, I can consciously over-ride this response and watch my mind and my ego relax along with my body. In the most ordinary terms, there is a universal design to the mechanical human body, shared by all healthy members of our species. Those who never lose it live with physical comfort and ease, aging without the typical structural collapse seen in so many elderly people in the "advanced" world. Learning these principles and putting them into practice in our daily lives is challenging for anyone. But the payoff is huge.

In terms of my own life, my body has become an anchor to the present moment as I've become more proficient at tuning inside, under my skin, and meditating on awareness of my body all day long, whatever I am doing. In this way, *when I am present enough to remember* (this is my biggest challenge) I return to what I once knew as a baby—how to fulfill the promise of my human existence, which is simply to *be* the miracle of embodied presence.

This understanding has had wide-ranging effects on so many aspects of my life. I am far less critical of others and of myself. When I am critical of myself, I just don't get caught there. I sometimes experience little "flashbacks" of things I have done or said throughout my life that were unkind or at least thoughtless or unconscious. There will sometimes be a little stab of remorse or mortification that comes with the memory, but when this happens, I find that I am able to recognize what I have learned from this, that I would never do or say that now, and then I can let it go. Whereas I might have once kept a mental scorecard of the wrongs perpetuated against me, that slate seems to have been wiped clean, and any admonishment that surfaces is for the ways in which I have been the one to be inconsiderate. I've wondered at times if I came into the world with a tendency to focus on the negative rather than the positive, remembering the slights instead of the kindnesses extended to me. I've wished I could have had these insights when my parents were still alive, but I also sense that in the greater scheme of things, it's really okay now just the way it is.

I also worry a lot less. When I do find myself worrying about something, I can see it as a state of mind that I am able to manage, that is driven by thoughts that might or might not be true, and that it is a worthless pastime. I don't have the kinds of expectations of people or events that I once had. I seem to be able to just take things as they come more of the time. Although I still feel mildly inadequate or unattractive at times, these thoughts are fleeting and don't stick like they once did.

I do feel pangs of disappointment at times when I look in the mirror and see a suddenly much older woman looking back at me. I must say, though, that I'm actually beginning to like the way she looks! The more the gray hair comes in and the deeper the wrinkles take hold, the more I find myself being willing to give myself over to the reality of this new way of being. This is a fairly recent shift. I watch people around me getting cosmetic surgery and doing multiple things to try to look younger than they really are, and I'm grateful not to be chasing that illusion anymore.

I hardly ever feel angry anymore (besides having strong opinions about political/social justice issues that I can get worked up about). Few people get on my nerves or cause me to be annoyed or feel disappointed. I like just about everyone I know or come into contact with. I appreciate people's individual styles and quirkiness now. At times, I am almost overcome by a sweeping, loving feeling when listening to or watching someone. I don't mind criticism anymore, and if I receive it, it seems appropriate and pretty much on the mark.

There's not much upheaval anymore around relationships. As a mother, I'm much less hovering or caught up in feeling responsible, and am better able to live a life that is more independent of my children, although I still long for greater geographic closeness with them so that we can be together more often.

In coming home to myself, I see that there are aspects that seem permanent in the sense of "this is who I am" and that is unchanging. But at the same time, "home" is not a destination that we ever completely reach—that would deny our need to remain conscious. It's a dynamic interplay between being settled and secure in who we are and at the same time, feeling fresh and renewed, and not taking anything for granted.

Joan Waite

Singing Her Own Song

Joan Waite was born in Toronto, Canada in 1933 out of wedlock to a twenty-four-year-old mother. These were shameful circumstances at the time, so to hide the reality of her situation, her grandmother, a homemaker, and her grandfather, a porter on the railroad, raised her. She grew up thinking they were her parents and her mother was her sister. It wasn't until she was thirteen years old that she learned the truth. It was a traumatic time for her and her mother. What stays in her mind is that her mother didn't hug her or show any real affection for her when she broke the news.

Her mother married when Joan was four, and she would spend the summers with her and her husband in the countryside near a lake. Of course, at the time, she still thought she was her sister. When she found out she was her birth mother at thirteen, she wanted to live with them, but they didn't want her. Instead, they took in a Native American foster child. At the time Joan didn't allow herself to feel any jealousy or anger that her mother was taking in someone else instead of her own daughter. It was only years later when she entered psychotherapy that Joan was able to face the anger and abandonment she had harbored for years.

As a black child in a white school and neighborhood, Joan grew up with a lot of prejudice and name-calling. When she entered high school, things improved. One of the few blacks in a white academic high school, she became class representative to the student organization and the first black cheerleader in Toronto in the 1940s. But still, the lines were drawn racially; white boys would never ask her out. But when a new black male student moved into the area her sophomore year, he became the captain of the football team, and they became a model black couple. They were both active in organizations and activities, so high school was a positive experience for her.

Joan had an aunt and uncle who had moved to the states and lived on Long Island; they helped her obtain a scholarship to Sarah Lawrence and, for the first time, shared the identity of her father with her. She spent four wonderful years in college, including a junior year abroad in France. At Sarah Lawrence, she began to study African cultures within the context of anthropology.

The next years were busy: she received a master's from Northwestern University in cultural anthropology, moved to New York, became a community organizer in East Harlem, and began to speak Spanish in addition to French and German that she had already learned. There she met her husband, a time-study engineer who was born and raised in Sierra Leone by black missionary parents.

After their first child was born, they headed to Nigeria—a dream come true for Joan—and they spent four years there. He organized and managed a plant that assembled radios for the first time in West Africa, and she did folk singing for a children's television program. Their second child was born there, and they had a third after they came home.

The last year in Nigeria Joan became very ill. She was totally exhausted and running a fever. No one could figure out what was wrong, so they came home to seek medical care. Test after test showed that there was no physical basis for her illness. She had to face the fact that it was a psychosomatic; repressing all her feelings about her past had made her sick. She needed psychotherapy to cope with the rage and feelings of abandonment she had buried inside all these years and thus began a healing process that would last for thirty years. Although she never returned to Canada, she did reflect many times on those early years that were instrumental in shaping the woman she has become today.

On her return to the states from Nigeria, she and her family moved to Teaneck, New Jersey, and she focused on raising her children and work. She developed a Saturday school for black children that addressed the achievement gap between blacks and whites and Asians; she taught "African Arts and their Transmission to the Americas" at Sarah Lawrence and became Director of Education for the African Art Museum of the SMA Fathers in Tenafly, New Jersey and on and on. Her work always centered on anthropology with an emphasis on Africa and African-Americans; at heart, she was more of a community organizer than an academician. When she wasn't working, she enjoyed listening to music and was always part of a choir.

In 1994, she and her husband, who had become a corporate vice president, retired and downsized to a townhouse in Princeton, New Jersey. As a retired couple, they enjoyed going to concerts all the time. The first time she heard the Westminster Jubilee Singers, she knew she had to audition for this choir. It is a multicultural, multiracial and interdenominational choral ensemble composed of students from Westminster Choir College of Rider University who perform selections of African and African American music. As she explains in her own words, joining this special choir changed her life: It touched her deeply and brought all her interests together. More importantly, it motivated her to sing solo.

Today at seventy-seven years of age with fifty-one years of marriage to her credit, Joan Waite's life revolves around practicing for and giving solo charity concerts. Hearing her resonant heart-felt voice, you know that this richness is emerging from someone who has found her own personal home: Joan Waite knows herself well, is content with who she has become, and is generous in sharing this hard-earned wisdom with others.

In her own words....

Since my grandparents colluded with my mother in saying that she was my sister and that they were my parents, I grew up referring to them in that way. When I saw evidences that this was not true, like church members referring to my grandmother as my "Grandmother" and not my mother, I ignored the reality, probably to protect myself from the pain of knowing that my mother had not wanted me. So on the surface, I was a happy kid and a highly achieving student but underneath, I had all these feelings that I didn't allow myself to acknowledge until I was much older.

One thing I do remember: even from the time I was a young girl, I wanted to excel and shine. Feeling abandoned, that was part of my motivation in so many things I did. I wanted to be the best person I could so I would be wanted and loved. When I was thirteen years old in the last year of elementary school, I received special commendation for an oration I gave on the topic of "Madame Marie Curie and Her Discovery of Radium."

I also had a strong desire to belong, which stimulated interest in my African American heritage and culture. At eighteen years of age I won an oratorical contest sponsored by our African American church for both U.S. and Canadian students in Fort Wayne, Indiana. My speech, on "The Contribution of the Negro to Civilization," earned me a scholarship to any college of my choice, which I added to the scholarship I received the same year from Sarah Lawrence College in Bronxville, New York.

When I arrived in the states, my aunt and uncle, who had facilitated my search for an American college, explained my father's identity to me. He was Richard Huey, a singer, songwriter, radio host and actor who had performed on Broadway. They gave me a book in which he appeared called *The Negro in American Theatre* and described how he had met my mother in Toronto when he had come to perform in a production of "Porgy and Bess," and she had joined the chorus of dancers. After a short tryst he had traveled on with the company to perform in London, England. He was never told the story of my birth.

Years later in my thirties, when my husband Bob and I attended a friend's party, I overheard two gentlemen reminiscing about the old days when Richard Huey had his radio show in New York. I didn't have the nerve to say anything then but after procuring the telephone number of one of these men, I called him to tell him who I was. He kindly invited me to his home, so he could tell me more about my father, now deceased. There I learned the name and address of Richard Huey's wife who lived not far from him.

After I had gathered enough courage to introduce myself to her in a letter, I was pleasantly surprised to receive a warm response and invitation to her home. She then told me I had a stepsister, the daughter of Richard Huey and a woman with whom he had lived for many years before his marriage to her. Bob and I drove with our children to Boston to meet my stepsister, and again, I was so happy to be warmly received and to know that in her words, "Our father would have loved you if he had known." What a wonderful revelation for me!

Back to my college years—they were a wonderful experience. I could focus on languages and anthropology and my special interest in Africa. When Bob and I had an opportunity to go to Africa, I was thrilled. Part of my wanting to go to Africa was to fill this need to be wanted as a result of being abandoned by my mother; Africa became a substitute. I did some research there in African arts, but I also had a big disappointment in Nigeria: I wanted to use my community organization skills to work for a social agency, but I couldn't get a job; an African friend told me that I was threatening because I was too well educated. That was a real bummer for me. I ended up recruiting international kids to do folk singing with me on Nigerian television.

Our last year in Nigeria I got very sick. In fact, I became so sick that we had to come home. At first they thought I had malaria but the aching body, severe fatigue and fevers persisted after I came home. I was "forced" by Bob and then by a psychotherapist to accept the fact that the symptoms were psychosomatic and gradually found that they were reflective of all the emotions associated with my abandonment—hurt, sadness, anger, and fear—that I had been repressing my whole life. After the first four years of therapy I was healed enough to accept an Associate Professorship at Sarah Lawrence College teaching "The Arts of Africa and Their Transmission to the New World." So I was able to function, but I was in therapy for close to thirty years.

Since Bob had been in therapy before we married, he was much more cognizant of its benefits than was I. After fifteen years with my first therapist, and a period of about five years after, I realized that I still had feelings of fear and a lack of self esteem that prohibited me from being my "true self," so I interviewed five new therapists and chose one who practiced group therapy.

The group, which I stayed with for another fifteen years, really helped me resolve my remaining problems, some of which were related to Bob, such as not standing up for myself, fearing to make demands, that kind of thing. Fortunately he was willing to come to "couples" sessions where we could both work on these issues and significantly improve our relationship. It was this process that contributed to our long marriage.

After the first job teaching at Sarah Lawrence, I held a number of positions over the next twenty years: mainly organizing and developing educational programs and teaching, all with an interest in Africa and African American heritage and culture.

Bob and I retired in 1994—I was sixty-one—and moved to Princeton because there's so much culture there. Once we got here, I said to myself, ok, now I can relax and do things for fun. One of the things we enjoy doing together is going to concerts. One day we went to Westminster Choir College in Princeton, which is comparable to the Julliard School of Music in New York, to hear their Jubilee Singers. This group is a mix of kids from different religious backgrounds and races but they perform African American spirituals and folk songs, classical music by African American composers, African chants and gospel music. When I heard them sing, I was floored. I was so excited. It was so great! I was thrilled to find a choir that wasn't just a choir but reached me very deeply with the music of Africans and African Americans that I loved so much.

After that first concert, I knew that this was the choir I wanted to sing with, and I had to take the risk of auditioning as a retired senior. This was a turning point for me and showed me how important it is to know yourself, to know what you want, and to be willing to take risks.

I went in and asked them if they accepted community people in the choir. Oh, no, they told me, this is a college choir. I told them that I'd sung with Collegiate Chorale founded by Robert Shaw in Manhattan. They didn't care. I kept pushing them. I finally called the choir director and told him my background. He said that the only way to be a part of the choir was to pay tuition, become a student and audition. So I paid the tuition of five hundred dollars for one credit, passed the audition and sang with the seventeen to twenty- year-olds. I did that for four years. They called me "Miss" Joan; I was the grandmother of the group and loved every minute of it.

After I was in the choir for two years, I wanted to sing solo, so I took voice lessons. I practiced an hour a day for two years. At the end of that time, I gave my first solo concert as a mezzo-soprano accompanied by a pianist, and I've been giving them ever since. This was totally unexpected. I just joined the choir because I enjoy singing African American music and out of my deep love for that music, a new passion arose.

As a younger woman, I enjoyed singing alone, often accompanying myself on the guitar or singing with other folk singers as we performed together (with the exception of a few solo performances on Nigerian TV). However, when I was younger, I had no desire to sing solos accompanied by piano, and I never did.

When I first started singing solo in my sixties, I struggled with having too high expectations for myself, so I had to relax and slowly move at a comfortable pace. I also had some performance anxiety, as you can imagine. I coped by learning to wait and center myself by breathing deeply before nodding to my piano accompanist to start playing.

Of course, I feel more relaxed when singing in a choir because I am not nearly as exposed if I were to make a mistake. In a choir if you're not sure of a note, you can let others cover it. As a soloist,

I am exposed and responsible for every note, which, of course, incurs anxiety. However, on the positive side, as a soloist I feel a much more direct connection with the audience as a whole as well as with specific individuals whom I see responding to my performance.

It's thrilling to give a solo concert. I take pleasure in the fact that people are enjoying it, and it gives me a sense of sharing. In all my concerts, I blend European art songs, Negro spirituals, Broadway show tunes, and jazz. For my last concert, "Travel the World in Song," I sang nineteen songs in twelve different languages from Europe, the Middle East, the Far East, India, West Africa, South Africa and the Americas. That's exciting for me. People in the audience realize that I'm respecting their cultures.

These concerts bring all my interests together: language, culture, and music. I give concerts annually, sometimes twice a year. In between I take time to learn the music. I'm doing this for enjoyment, not because I have to earn a living, which is so wonderful, although my husband teases me that the way I work at it and drive myself, I could be making money! Today I continue to take voice lessons and practice an hour each day.

I feel blessed to have the opportunity to do this. These solo concerts are also meaningful to me because I offer them as benefits for charitable organizations, allowing me to give back for all the opportunities I have had. The last concert, performed in two different venues, raised four thousand dollars for The Trenton Soup Kitchen and three thousand dollars for The Crisis Ministry of Princeton and Trenton.

I lived with a feeling of abandonment for decades and it took years of psychotherapy to deal with it. Through this process, I learned to experience and respect my own feelings and to recognize and express my anger. And I got it all out!

As a result of my experience in therapy, I've been able to accept who I am, honor the talent I have, and relax and enjoy it without having to be anything else. For a while I thought I had to get that doctorate. I was measuring my success by social or academic standards as opposed to who I was as a person. My solo singing completes my coming home to myself: I am content with who I am, and I'm doing what I love. And as an added bonus, the roar of applause reassures me, at long last, that I am valued and loved.

Valerie Ramsey

Living Life in Reverse

An only child whose parents divorced when she was four, Valerie Ramsey, seventy, wanted nothing more than to have a typical childhood where the whole family ate meat loaf and mashed potatoes together and her parents sat next to her on the sofa watching "Leave it to Beaver" on television in the evening. But that was not meant to be. After her parents' divorce, Valerie and her mother moved in with her maternal grandparents, who lived in Westchester County, New York.

Her grandfather, a successful businessman, had built cement plants all over South America, so her mother had grown up in Buenos Aires and Rio. Her mother loved the glamour of travel and began her own career working for Pan American airlines in the 1940s, when it was unusual for women to have high-profile careers. Pan Am was building Intercontinental Hotels in South America and asked her mother to travel with their president and his team to help them establish these hotels.

Because her mother traveled so much, she enrolled Valerie in a coed boarding school in New Rochelle, New York at the age of seven, and she spent the weekends at her grandparents. She missed her mother a lot but slowly, she formed a family of friends. Out of necessity, she became self-reliant, and by the time she graduated from an all-girls boarding high school, she was head of the chapel committee, a regular on the school's self-government committee and ran half the school's intramural team.

Valerie wanted to go to college in California —she was tired of the northeast—but her mother refused to send her there because that is where her father, who had remarried, lived. She feared they'd get too close. Instead Valerie entered Rollins College in Winter Park, Florida at age seventeen. The first week of college she met her future husband, Wally. A handsome, older man (by seven years), he had just completed four years in the Air Force and was ready to settle down. Valerie completed two years of college before she and Wally became engaged, then at her mother's insistence, spent a summer in secretarial school learning to type and take shorthand before getting married. Soon after, she landed a job as an executive assistant at MCA, a large theatrical agency headquartered in New York City and LA. Her mother felt very strongly that a young woman needed to have experience holding down a job before she married, saying that you never knew what life might hand you, and you should always have a skill to fall back on.

Valerie and Wally married when she was just twenty. Although Wally had grown up in a traditional, intact household, he, too, was an only child. They were both determined to create the big, noisy family they had yearned for as children. When Wally got a job teaching ninth grade English at Greenwich Country Day School, they were able to live on campus, and their children received free tuition. Within nine years, they had six children.

Valerie loved being a full-time mother. She could do all the things she wished her mother had done: She attended her children's school plays and recitals, threw elaborate dinner parties for the other faculty families, took family vacations to Florida in the winter and let her kids sleep in front of the fireplace in their sleeping bags during ice storms. But in the back of her mind, she knew that she'd still be young when her children left home and looked forward to the day when she could have an effect on the real world through her own career.

Before she knew it, all the children had left the nest and were scattered across the country. She and Wally had grown to love California from their annual visits to see her mother and stepfather, who had relocated in Carmel years ago, and so they decided to move to southern California. It was 1987 and Valerie was forty-eight years old.

"When we moved, I knew this was my big opportunity. I wanted to make a mark for myself in the corporate world," she told me. "I wanted a real identity, a career I could be proud of and grow in."

Valerie was drawn to the hospitality industry, probably because that had been her mother's field. The only place she applied for a job was Pebble Beach Resorts, an exclusive resort about a hundred miles south of San Francisco. They hired her to work in the pro shop selling golf balls with the college kids. Within four years, she had worked her way up to Public Relations and Media Manager for the entire resort (three hotels, four golf courses, nine restaurants, a large spa, and the famous Seventeen-Mile Drive).

In the first three days in her new position, she broke her foot, sprained her ankle, and was diagnosed with uterine cancer and a serious heart condition. This was a monumental turning point: Should she fold her tent and go home or decide that these setbacks were not going to stop her from achieving her dream?

Without a moment's hesitation, Valerie decided to move forward despite serious medical problems. As she explains in the next section, once she addressed these issues, all sorts of doors have opened for her. At age sixty-three, she was discovered as a model. The average model begins her career between the ages of twelve and eighteen and works until her late twenties or early thirties. When Valerie was a teenager, she admired the models in *Seventeen* magazine, thinking how much fun it would be to wear beautiful clothing and travel to exotic locations for photo shoots, but she knew her parents would never approve. In her twenties and thirties as a young mother, modeling wasn't even a blink on her horizon.

Valerie Ramsey lived her life in reverse of most women: raising her family was her first homecoming and then forging into the corporate world, striking out on her own and discovering her many talents brought her home for a second time. In the last ten years, she has co-authored and published a book, *Gracefully: Looking and Being Your Best at Any Age*, launched a speaking career, and is in the process of developing two national television shows. From a stay-at-home mother of six to a career woman to a runway model, Valerie has said a wholehearted "Yes" to life at every turning point of her development. Five feet, ten inches tall with a stunning shock of silver white hair, Valerie has the looks to turn heads and the energy and drive that women half her age envy. In the following section, she shares the process of her journey.

In her own words....

I turned seventy last week, and I've been in a celebratory mood ever since. I thought I'd be bummed out about it, but I feel rejuvenated and excited, because I have so many great projects on my plate. My first homecoming was having a happy brood of a family. That was expected. What *wasn't* expected was the second homecoming when we moved from Connecticut to California, and I found my second true calling.

I wanted a challenging and interesting career in the corporate world, one where I could learn new skills, work with a big organization, and experience teamwork. And I wanted a real salary with benefits; it felt like a challenge. When my children were little I worked part-time in a retail store, then I got an associate degree in interior design and worked part-time as a decorator. But I had never worked full-time. Now, I wanted a real identity, one that I could be proud of, a career that I could grow in.

I loved raising the children, but I knew that wouldn't last forever. I'd still be young when they left. We were a great, close-knit family. But as they got into high school, I kept wondering: what's the next step for me? I wasn't the type to do volunteer work and play bridge. I had no intention of working when the children were at home. It is my belief that if you have children, you owe it to them to be home with them and be the best parent you can possibly be. When they were born, I wouldn't even hire a baby nurse.

My mother and stepfather moved to Carmel the year our youngest child was born. We'd visit them on school vacations. It's one of the most beautiful parts of the country, just a spectacular area. We moved out here the year my mother got cancer—1987; sadly, she passed away before we arrived.

When we got out to California, I knew this was my big opportunity. I always believed that women could do anything they wanted to do.

My mother was a tremendous role model for that. She was a stylish woman who grew up in the world of hospitality. She was raised all over South America. She went swimming with Evita Peron!

The only place I wanted to work was Pebble Beach Resorts. I longed for that same glamour my mother had enjoyed. I liked the idea of working in hospitality, especially out here at Pebble Beach. I knew I wanted a career, but I didn't know what the career would be; I thought being a concierge would be fun. I knew I wanted to grow beyond that, but I wasn't certain what opportunities would entice me. The Human Resources Department suggested that I work in the pro shop first so I could learn about the resort. I was fine with that.

I started at an entry-level job that didn't require a lot of experience. I had worked in retail before, and I felt comfortable dealing with the public. You do one thing and then move up and take the next step. While I was working in the pro shop, I also went to the local community college and learned how to use a computer. From retail, I moved up to marketing. It was a small department that also handled public relations and advertising. I started out as an administrative assistant and was able to put my new computer skills to good use. I was very nervous then, but it's never as scary as you think it will be. People make the learning process easier for you. In spite of my worse fears, it was fine.

For four years I supported the top executives in the department. Then, when the public relations and media manager left, I went in to the senior vice president and asked for her job. He gave it to me on the spot.

That first week on the job was a major turning point in my life. I had a film crew up from LA filming a Cadillac commercial. Golfers were teeing off every ten minutes. It was a big staging job. That first morning, I was to meet them on the seventh hole. It was five a.m., misty and dark, and I was running out to meet them on the cart path. I stumbled and fell flat on my face, breaking my foot and spraining my ankle. I was really in pain. Instead of Miss Capability, I felt just like Calamity Jane.

The second day I arrived at the shoot on crutches. I was with the Cadillac people when my doctor called on my cell: I had uterine cancer from the tests he had run the week before. He was scheduling a complete hysterectomy. For the third day in a row, I left early. When I saw the doctor, he listened to my heart and said something was seriously wrong. He set up a consult with a cardiologist. I had a very serious case of cardiomyopathy, which causes a kind of arrhythmia that can send you into cardiac arrest.

I had surgery for the uterine cancer; that took care of it all. I had a defibrillator implanted under my pectoral muscle and was put on a new state-of-the-art heart medication. It was believed that a cold virus had gotten into the heart muscle causing the condition. If it didn't get better, I would need a heart transplant. Fortunately, in my case, it kept getting better and better.

The first three days in my new job, and I'm down three for three. It was a scary time: That put me to the test. I thought, I'm fifty-eight, oh boy, is this a sign that I shouldn't do this, that I've taken on too much? I thought, gosh darn it now, I really want this. It's a bump in the road, not the *end* of the road.

I don't give up easily. This was my dream job. I knew I could make something out of it, and I firmly believed I'd get though the cancer and everything would be all right. I decided I wasn't going to give up on my dream; I would do what had to be done and get though it.

And I'm so glad I did. I've always had a positive attitude. That's how I got through boarding school and summers with my dad. It was so heart wrenching to say goodbye to my mother and stepfather; I adored them. Summers with my father and stepmother were rough: they were both very cold and judgmental. Nothing you did was ever good enough. It was an uncomfortable environment, but I persevered.

I got through the surgeries and got back on track. The job was moving along nicely. Now I'm sixty-three, on the golf course with a Hollywood producer and film crew when the producer tells me he wants to recommend me to the biggest modeling agency in San

Francisco. I thought he was joking. Two days later, they signed me up and that launched my modeling career.

But I didn't give up my day job; I loved it too much—the people, the challenges, the sense of accomplishment, just the pride and fun in working for such a world class resort! I stayed for another five years until a local newspaper came to me and said their readers would love to hear my story, to see how I lived life in reverse. The article was picked up by the national newswires, and soon I began receiving emails from women all over the United States. Many told me they found my story so inspiring, that they thought their life was over at fifty or sixty, that they had thought there were no new challenges or dreams left for them to pursue, and that I'd given them hope.

I read the emails to my daughter, Heather, who's a writer. She said, "Mom, you have the basis for a book." My daughter put together a proposal for a how-to book for women over forty on how to look and feel your best at any age. Within forty-eight hours, we had an agent. Two weeks later, McGraw Hill agreed to publish it. The editor there is a young man, thirty-five. It was so validating that a young man "got" it. If the editor were another sixty-five-year-old woman, of course she'd get it. The book came out in May 2008. That led to TV appearances including a third appearance on the Today show, Neil Cavuto's Fox Business News, Extra and many others. Soon Premiere Speakers Bureau recruited me.

When *Gracefully* came out I was sixty-eight. I decided it was time to leave my wonderful job at Pebble Beach; I'd been there fifteen years. I knew there would be new doors opening, and I wanted to be free to walk through them. The opportunities just keep pouring in: a New York fashion designer asked me to be an ambassador for her. I wear her clothes and travel for her. You Go Girls Travels asked me to be an ambassador for their company, which caters to women who want to travel but don't want to travel alone. They put together an unforgettable trip to Paris to celebrate our new relationship.

I have two TV projects in development: One is called "What's Next?" In it I will interview people all over country about transitions they are going through, ways they are making changes in their lives. We'll shoot in great locations with real life people.

I am also a frequent speaker for the American Heart Association and give a lot of keynotes speeches at the Go Red for Women fund-raisers.

My life just keeps getting bigger and better. I've never felt so excited or so invigorated. My feeling is wow, I've just turned seventy. That's a *real* reason to celebrate! Everyday I meet the greatest people. I'm amazed at the wonderful world of networking. People put themselves out there to help me. It's just astounding.

I do have to make an effort to keep my energy paced. My stamina doesn't always keep up with my internal engine, but my health issues are under control. My kids are all successful and happy in their own lives. Wally is so supportive; he loves everything I'm doing. He's happy to take me to the airport, but he doesn't come on every trip. He's very self-sufficient and always has projects going at home.

This year is our fiftieth wedding anniversary. Our closest friends are all still married too. Years ago, divorce wasn't the option that it seems to be today. There was such a strong sense of commitment. We had realistic expectations: we were wise enough to know it wouldn't be perfect all the time. With six children, we didn't think about breaking up the family. You just tightened your belt and got through it. There was a sense of cooperation and of being a team. You pick your battles. You ask, is it important? Will it matter next week? You have a sense of humor and patience. Wally and I enjoy doing things together, we laugh at the little things, and we have the same values, of course.

At seventy years of age, I'm comfortable with who I've become and have the freedom to live my truth. I'm doing the things that most fulfill my passion: inspiring other women to continue to grow, to expand their horizons, and to reinvent themselves as they move through transitions, especially aging. I firmly believe we're never too old to have a new dream or to celebrate a new success, and my life is proof of that.

I was shy as a child. Growing up in boarding schools, I never felt secure even though I did gain a tremendous sense of independence. I couldn't run home to my mommy when my feelings were hurt. In the last fifteen years, I have completely come out of my shell and found my place in the world. No longer shy at all, I embrace life, new opportunities, and all of the incredible people that I meet along the way. I'm filled with excitement and gratitude, appreciating today and filled with high anticipation for tomorrow.

Piper Leigh

Connection and Creativity

For years, artists have been drawn to the light, colors and spaciousness of Northern New Mexico. The most famous of those artists, Georgia O'Keeffe, knew she had found her spiritual home after spending just one summer there. Twenty years later she moved permanently and remarked, "I never feel at home in the East like I do out here. I feel like myself and I like it."

Similarly, Piper Leigh, a poet, book artist and photographer who is a consultant to groups and communities, was attracted to the stark desert beauty of the southwest. Piper grew up in a traditional, corporate family and until she moved to Santa Fe, had not lived in one place for more than five years. Born in the Texas panhandle, she lived in southern California, Dallas, upstate New York and Kansas City all briefly. With so many moves as a child and young adult, she couldn't trust her environment: she didn't know when she'd need to pick up and move again. She yearned to stay in one place long enough to develop a close friend. One positive aspect to all the moves was that her parents, brother and she became "a small circle of four." Holidays, like Christmas and Halloween, were grand celebrations no matter where they lived with lots of decorations, candles, and singing. They shared the details of each other's lives as if their lives depended on this knowledge, because to others, they were unknowns without a history.

In August of 1982, after separating from her first husband, Piper moved to Santa Fe, New Mexico. After a lifetime of temporary homes, she had no expectations that this move would be permanent. But she felt an immediate connection. Like Georgia O'Keeffe, she fell in love with the light and desert colors, the warmth and the mountains. The physical presence of the place was so powerful that she allowed herself to sink roots for the very first time. This sensory homecoming inspired her to seek her true self and come home on many different levels. She has been in Santa Fe ever since.

Her first job in Santa Fe was in the unlikely world of commercial banking (Formerly she had worked for a nonprofit). At the bank, her interest in how people work together took the form of training, management and marketing. When the bank was sold, she worked for an experiential education school, Santa Fe Mountain Center, managing its organizational development program. There she took learning out of the conference room and into the wilderness. Drawing on the power and challenge of the wilderness she created brief, intensive learning communities that served as laboratories for organizational learning. "In all my work situations I was drawn to community, to look at how people work together and how they become connected to community," she told me. "I didn't seek this work but was drawn to it by the importance of finding community in my own life."

In 1993, she and her new husband, whom she worked with at the Mountain Center, formed their own business to help organizations and people learn from each other and see their business issues in a different light. Rather than acting as the experts, Piper and her husband facilitate conversations and learning, so people and organizations can find their own solutions to problems.

When Piper is not working with groups, she is in her studio office writing poetry and hand crafting books. She has been involved with poetry since she was in graduate school, often writing with groups of women poets. For many years she created "palm" books (that fit into the palm of your hand) or other small works she'd send out through the mail to her friends. No one had to respond; she simply enjoyed sending them out and making a connection. More recently, she creates email "postcards" of her poems and images that she emails to friends and colleagues. She has also sold her handmade artist books to a local gallery, shown them at book art exhibits, and published her poems in local literary magazines.

Piper is part of several poetry groups. One of her colleagues, who suggested I include Piper in this book project, had this to say about Piper's poetry: "Reading Piper's poetry is like looking through a diaphanous curtain. A dreamlike quality pervades her work, speaking to a deep spirituality and understanding of other worlds. Once into the poem, you realize there may be two or three other stories, all woven with such a deft hand that it is hard to separate the realities. Piper takes you into the damp places of the soul."

Interestingly, our conversations have created ripples throughout Piper's work. She feels that our interviews have strengthened her commitment to her poetry and art as well as to solitude and community. Insights about the connection between landscape, art and home were already emerging in her work, and our discussions have heightened her awareness of the dynamics among these three and the practices that nurture a joyful, courageous creative life—a life which she hopes will, in turn, serve the world in unexpected ways.

For the last three years, Piper has been studying Buddhism with a learned teacher. Although she had done reading in the past, this is the first time she is practicing and sitting as part of a community. She says, "This is another coming home, another commitment. It's like we're travelers, and we create a refuge and home with each other in the continuity of our study and practice."

In her study of Buddhism and in other ways, Piper has been pushing against convention, trying to find her own way. Longing for community, a place of permanence she could trust, and a voice of her own, she came to the southwest. The move was pivotal in her journey of actualizing herself. In Santa Fe, she found a connection to the land, a community she could trust, a voice in her poetry and art, and a supportive husband who shared her values. For the first time in her life, Piper Leigh, fifty-six, feels that she has found her true home and that she belongs. What follows is a poem by Piper Leigh and her reflections on her journey home.

J'ai Bleu de Toi
(I'm Crazy in love with you)

My life has been a series of falls.

Nana fell down the blue grey
stairs, no broken bones, but her bruises,
dark petunias, seeped into my five
year old skin. Standing on the porch,
I watched my mother's foot
catch on the split puckered cement.
I flew to her. Too late.

In December, bundled in a thick coat
and scarf, I watched Niagara tumble
through ice. I watched, voiceless,
unable to save my uprooted family.

My brother fell over and over
inside football, marriage, large
dreams. My father bought life insurance
on his frail heart, but Mother died instead
falling away from his grasp.

My first love threw me empty
into New England's frozen landscape.
I fell out of the East into a desert

where broken wings heal,
bones dry to white beauty,
geography demands the truth.

I rise, j'ai bleu de toi, in Capulin Canyon.

Piper Leigh, August 2005

In her own words....

This land of New Mexico feels like home though it's nothing like I ever experienced. Separating from my marriage, I needed a shift to someplace totally different. New England was beautiful and picture perfect: white picket fences, steepled churches, a long history. Yet I felt like I was drowning in my husband's darkness and in my own loneliness – it was this heaviness from which I wanted to break away.

Driving out to New Mexico, a landscape I had never seen, was a huge risk. I did it without knowing, without a plan. It provided an unexpected awakening. There was a big sky and no fences, it was gloriously messy and had a kind of wildness that I had never lived in. There were people who had lived here for many generations and many people who were not from here. Perhaps even misfits. People didn't ask for credentials or history to qualify your place in this community.

I had moved so many times as a child. My happiest years were from fifth to eighth grade. Not surprisingly, this was when my father didn't travel. No goodbyes. My most painful move came at age thirteen. I was in the ninth grade when we moved to Kansas City, where we lived in the suburbs, which I hated, and I graduated in a class of nine hundred. After attending a small college, I did graduate work in Madison, Wisconsin, and married a medical student. He was a gentle, quiet young man who taught me there could be relationship and presence without chatter and so much effort. We had an easy, loving acceptance between us, and grew up together. We both wanted a life that was not suburban or materialistic.

During his residency, we lived in western Massachusetts. I felt like I didn't have a place there: I was caught between the value of family and the concept of marriage as an old and limited view of relationship and certainly not always healthy for women. Our marriage extended my family and created a larger circle, which pleased me. My family would not be able to link to my relationship and life if I hadn't been married. And yet my husband and I wondered if we had "sold out," if we should have taken a stand against the institution of marriage that seemed to be crumbling and was often full of secrets. How could I bc baking bread, weaving, playing the dulcimer and having babies in a rural community and also change the role of women in the world? The contradictions were painful and confusing.

Because I moved so much, I always yearned to belong to a community. As a young woman, I envisioned that rural picture for myself that I just mentioned. That never happened, and the sense of longing continued. I did belong to a community of women writers when I lived in Massachusetts, but the stay there was brief. Married to a doctor, I moved where he needed to do his residency. Eventually his depression began to seep into me. I knew I had to leave.

When we separated, I came to Santa Fe. When I first moved here, I didn't have a community yet, so I'd import my family for the holidays. I longed for community. My parents loved the small town feeling here, and that art and music were so easily available. After I had been here awhile, I invited friends to join our family holiday celebrations — the circle becoming bigger and more diverse. The simple traditions of *Las Posadas* and walks on Canyon Road at Christmas Eve were easy to join. July Fourth pancake breakfast and bandstand music in the Plaza, another example of old-fashioned community events, still delights my father. And they appreciate the home and extended circle of friends I've developed over the years.

My mother's way to maintain relationships despite our multiple moves was to write Christmas cards to many people all over the country. She maintained that list with incredible passion! I tried to follow her example, but I felt weighted down by those obligations. What if I let them go? I began to trust that my web of connections would change and shift, whether I wrote those cards or not.

My mother spent so much of her time wanting to fit in and looking for safety. She was a reluctant corporate wife. She was never disrespectful and certainly supported my father and his work, but I felt there was always something she resented and resisted in the expectations of conformity and conservatism. She wore rich, colorful scarves and loved putting accessories together, although she hardly spent any money on her own clothing. She never had spa treatments or joined the country club. Although she contributed hours and loving attention volunteering for the church, she balked at the assumption that women would do the work while the men in the church were in leadership roles "doing the thinking."

When I became a young feminist rebelling and criticizing so much of her role, I learned that she shared much of my point of view but never believed she could reject her role in the harsh manner I recommended. Relationships and community were too important to her. I think she feared she would be ostracized and isolated, and she was probably right. The price would have been too great for her.

Yet I understand how who *she* was has contributed to who *I* am. I come from a long line of women involved in hand work. My mother and grandmothers stitched, embroidered, crocheted and knitted. I don't cook or bake, but I make books and print my poems and photographs on fabrics, like this sheer blue kimono I made that has a poem and image stamped on it.

The kimono is transparent and transparency speaks to me: It's a synthesis of cloth and texture that tells of the permeability of different worlds and multiple experiences. Those years while I was in high school in a suburban environment, there were no permeable boundaries and little diversity. I believe you can choose between a culture of separation and one of connection. I love offering those choices to others and seeing what happens in a group where people are so sure they're different from others, and they're not. We're all linked.

I've always had wonderful older women friends. Those women have had an artistic orientation, and they are a strong support for my nontraditional choices. I've also had superb teachers who modeled a woman's voice for me. I wrote some poetry in grad school, in groups, and still do in the company of other women. A kind of alchemy occurs when I write in the presence of other women. There is a field that's created when we drop into the unknown together and then witness the unexpected, spontaneous discoveries that emerge from that journey. I hear the scratch of pen and then, each other's voices immediately after writing. I listen to my own voice in the weave of others. We are each touched and touch each other. It's an amazing experience.

Grounding myself in one place, I found that my voice surfaced. Before I didn't feel I had a voice: That was connected to my belief that I didn't belong. When I moved here, something different happened. I was immediately drawn to the space and the large scale of the landscape. I loved the spaciousness; I felt a connection here instantly.

I had no expectations; I didn't have a vision. I just came. My family wasn't oriented to the natural world. My mother's way of creating home was with the house, not the land. We never had a direct bond to place, because we moved so often. When I moved here, it was a leap of faith, encouraged by an old friend. I experienced a real sense of cutting loose from everything I knew.

Here, the landscape took over. I didn't know this would happen. Remaining detached was an impossibility. I had no idea how important the landscape was to me: the big, open sky, the messiness, the juxtaposition of things. It spoke to me and allowed me to develop a different relationship to a place and to my story.

Wilderness and being in the landscape opened up another world. What began to happen in my writing was that the inner and outer landscapes were in play and they informed each other: what I brought to the experience and what I experienced through it. I was writing about place, high desert and my story within that context.

I felt like I was growing roots for the first time in my life. This was a direct experience: being in it, not being an observer. When you sleep on the earth, you sense you belong to the land. I was responding to something I couldn't articulate, yet I felt the most unexpected joy. This place allowed me to find my own way. Like me, a lot of people piece together their lives here. I am very grateful that I came to a place with lots of possibilities for composing a new life.

When you move so often, there are lots of beginnings and endings but you never feel accepted. To be here and to learn to trust was new: to let myself feel a sense of belonging. There's a gift of being in one place over time and a place with such incredible history! I love ritual and there are so many here related to the seasons: The Day of the Dead, the *farolitas* at Christmas, the pilgrimage to Chimayo on Good Friday. All these rituals occur every year and provide a continuity of place and a rhythm. People in cities have less opportunity for this.

I've come to know myself and trust my own voice out of my direct experience with the land. I've been very fortunate to go on long Grand Canyon river trips. I like to feel the ground under my feet and gain confidence when I sleep under an open sky or carry a heavy pack. Something happened in the wilderness that helped me find my place. I'm not sure how it worked. It's not fixed but dynamic and changing. I moved into new territory—back-country skiing, hiking, camping. These were life-altering experiences. I was part of something bigger. I learned what was mine in the midst of a changing, unpredictable, overwhelming environment.

Many of my recent poems have the theme of finding my ground, standing my ground, or pilgrimage. My voice is always connected to the land, a metaphor linked to place, to the physical beauty and the power in that. It does feel like a coming together, a new definition of belonging.

My poetry continues to have the quality of a mysterious journey, one that explores and expresses connections and intersections between everyday and a larger view — between those inner and outer landscapes I mentioned. The play and synthesis of photographs, images, different book forms, and textures delights me. The physical container created for the words informs the poems and vice versa.

I've played music and danced but those were performance pieces, and I've always kept journals. When I began making books, the pieces came together. Something loosened and surfaced. Poetry is about discovery, about listening to a different voice. It feels like coming home: It's an honoring, an appreciating of my voice, and a looking back and seeing the themes. I'm a weaver of connections of seemingly unrelated things. That feels like I'm being who I am.

Trusting and valuing my voice results in a different definition of safety, unlike my mother's need for physical safety. It's *my* experience, and I'm speaking from that. My experience and my story, while not unique, form a unique composition. My best and truest voice is spoken from a place that's not preplanned, that's spontaneous. I learned that from the wilderness: The river is never the same. Likewise, I can't prepare for every experience. Voice is connected to the spontaneous part I allow to emerge. It's what happens in the moment. It's the same with art—you step into the unknown, something arises and you dance with it. It happens in the landscape and with writing.

Writing poetry and putting my poems into handmade books are ways to honor my voice, though I wish I'd found it earlier. In my generation of feminists, there was a lot of picking and choosing and testing and pushing away. I don't know what younger women do today.

I wish I'd taken my artwork more seriously at a younger age, and allowed myself the commitment for that. But at a younger age, I was responding to externals, to what's on the outside. I have a sense that some of this change is aging. In my forties there was a lot of pushing to get things done. Now, I don't want to push in that way. The last ten years I'm starting to make choices. How can I best offer what I have? And what supports that and what doesn't?

As my own voice becomes clearer, I want to help others find theirs. That's why I'm drawn to creating environments for people to have conversations. Whether art or poetry, I keep circling around to the same theme: how does conversation and experience create a meaning in the community and with yourself?

Now, I'm figuring out how the pieces fit together and what they mean. My husband and I formed our own business in 1993 to help organizations and people learn together, create new possibilities, and develop leadership. We help them find their own solutions and bring out the best in who they are.

I'm called a consultant, but what I really do is create the environment for people to engage, inquire, invent and build strong commitments to action. I teach the skills and practices of productive, creative conversation. These forums help people and organizations dream and invent together. My work encourages a creative orientation instead of a reactive orientation; much of this I have learned and practiced in my own life and art.

I also have a new home of a more spiritual nature. For the last three years, I've studied with a Buddhist teacher. I had read teachers like Pima Chodron, but I hadn't been part of a practicing community until now. I'm looking at how the practice and study of meditation informs my life and how my life informs my practice and study.

This very much has a feeling of coming home. My Buddhist teacher is a writer, who has developed a practice that incorporates traditional Zen practices and texts with new approaches to build community and action in the world—a kind of a "re-imagining of the Zen koan tradition." It encourages the kind of collective inquiry and conversation I ascribe to in writing and in my work with groups. This community or *sangha* is another circle in my life and results in the same kind of alchemy I experience in writing in the presence of others. I'm so grateful for this group at this time in my life. I don't know if I would have appreciated it at a younger age.

Everyone talks of the "zest" after menopause. What zest? I'm a long way into menopause but I'm not feeling the zest. A lot of it is learning to rest. There were times I couldn't move fast enough, but as I get older, I don't have the same energy. But I don't quite trust being tired either. I fear that if I rest, I won't be able to go back into the world. In the last five years, I'm choosing to spend more time alone, exploring the ebb and flow of things. I actually can't get enough time to myself. I trust now that people will still be there when I come back.

I'm aware of the preciousness of time as well as its limits. I have only so much time and energy: Where do I want to put it? I grew up with the belief that productivity, care for others, action, and busyness were the ingredients that would ensure that you were loved and valued, especially if you didn't have children.

Fortunately I found ways to explore new territory outside this definition of a meaningful life. My curiosity about how we "compose our lives," as Mary Catherine Bateson said, has led me to continue to expand that definition and find ways to integrate the inner and outer worlds and to allow myself to move back and forth between those spheres. Creativity's source is in stillness, wandering and play. I continue to learn how to choose quiet and solitude in the midst of our very active, demanding world. And I'm learning to trust that this settling as well as stirring the pot will serve the world. This is settling in a good way: Settling in not knowing it all and coming from places I love that give me joy. I trust that now; I used to think it was all luck.

Now I'm beginning to think about my legacy. What is my body of work? Can I trust my own voice and my own rhythm? You slow down, and other people will slow down with you. That's an honoring of who we are, of our gifts. Those feel like legacies.

Not having children makes the legacy question really powerful for me. Women I know who have daughters have a different experience: seeing parts of themselves at different times, the reverberations, what rises out of that. I have a tiny bit of that with my nieces. But it's my connections to people and my value in the world that matter to me.

Because I didn't have children I felt like I had to do really important work and consequently, work became more important. But someone told me, whether you have children or not, you grieve. If you have children, you grieve for the work life you didn't have, and if you don't have children, you grieve for the mother's life. Either way, there's something you mourn for and there's a gift. This was an important insight for me because most people pity you if you don't have children and treat you as less than a woman.

My gift may be to help others find their place, their voice and their creativity in the world. That's a kind of legacy.

This community is rich with vibrant, creative women. They show me that beauty can emerge at any stage of our lives, and especially as we age. These are women who have composed unusual and yet grounded lives, women who carefully consider the choices and decisions they face, and who support each other in their creative work and lives. We are witnesses and examples for each other. We celebrate and actively support each other's exploration and joyful expression. I am not burdened with the rules of appropriateness and obligation that limited my mother's life.

This amazing place has enabled me to come home to my true self. Writing and art are ways of listening to myself and hearing myself. Coming from my family of origin where I moved every five years, I couldn't trust the land and I couldn't trust that people would be there for me. Moving to Santa Fe was a turning point: I was able to break away from the traditional life of my childhood, establish a new sense of safety internally, create the community I longed for, and express my deepest self through my poetry and handmade books.

Joyce Kendall Friedman

A Return to Her Roots

Joyce Kendall Friedman has led an interesting life. Even though her father descended from two lineages of Orthodox Jewish rabbis, she grew up without a strong Jewish identity. Trained and educated as a scientist, she led a secular life for years but as she got older, knew that something was missing from her life. Exploring different religions and spiritual centers, she stumbled on Chasidic Judaism and felt for the first time in her life, that she had come home.

Home for her grandparents was Hungary. They came to the states in the early 1900s and settled in Bayonne, New Jersey where her father, Samuel, was raised with his three brothers and one sister, two of whom became lawyers. Even though her father was aware of his Orthodox Jewish heritage, he did not practice his faith until his final years. Like many Jewish immigrants in the early 1940s, he wanted to hide his heritage and assimilate in order to be safe from discrimination, so he left New Jersey to go to Hollywood with his friend Ozzie Nelson, whom he had met in law school. They had big plans to take their band to the stars.

Driving West on Route 66, redheaded Samuel changed his name to Jimmy Murphy and met Joyce's mother, a petite college student with porcelain skin and long black hair, who was waiting tables in a café in western Oklahoma. She was raised as a Nazarene—a religion that shuns smoking, drinking and dancing—and had no idea that because *her* grandmother was Jewish, that meant that she was too.

Joyce's mother was about to head to California to chaperone a girlfriend who planned to marry her sweetheart in Hollywood before he went off to war. When they arrived there, Joyce's father, who had arrived earlier, put her mother up in a Hollywood rooming house where the starlets stayed. Not surprisingly, they fell in love: a handsome older man (by eleven years) and a beautiful, naïve coed from Hydro, Oklahoma, population four hundred thirty-five.

Before their 1942 marriage, her father joined the army and changed his last name back to Friedman. From reading her mother's diary, Joyce believes that she was conceived in Paradise (!), a resort at the foot of Mount St. Helen's. He was stationed in Fort Lewis, Washington at first so he took his pregnant wife home to his Orthodox Jewish parents in New Jersey. Everyone assumed she was not Jewish, but her mother-in-law accepted her into her kosher kitchen anyway. Joyce was born in Jersey City, and they stayed there until she was six weeks old, when they flew to California to live with Joyce's aunt until her father returned from the war.

Joyce's father was in the service for ten years. His family followed him to Baltimore, Albuquerque, and also spent five years in Germany where her younger sister and brother were born. She remembers that her father would bring people liberated from the concentration camps to their house in Germany but was too young to understand who they were.

They returned to New Jersey in 1952 after her father left the service and pooled their money with other family members to buy a roofing company in Allentown, Pennsylvania, where Joyce spent her high school years. From the time she was ten years old until she left home at eighteen, her family spent many weekends in Bayonne, New Jersey with her grandparents, observing the Sabbath and holy days. Although she didn't know it at the time, these weekends had a profound impact on her. The rest of the time her family didn't engage in religious activity, although her brother did have a Bar Mitzvah.

There was no money for college, so Joyce went to Kansas City to airline school and became a reservation agent. She was stationed at Idlewild Airport (now JFK) in New York. During this time, she married a meteorologist in the Air Force but ended the marriage after a year when she realized they had nothing in common. In Kansas City and New York City, she'd go to synagogue occasionally, but it wasn't a spiritual experience for her. Going to college was always her goal, so while stationed in Kansas City, she began taking night courses at a junior college. After two years with TWA, she quit and moved to Oklahoma City, where her mother had settled after her divorce.

Joyce considered her mother a very spiritual person, because she always had some kind of spiritual underpinnings to her life. She read Edgar Cayce and sought out mediums or rabbis who were mediums. Although her mother only attended synagogue occasionally, she felt attached to Judaism throughout her marriage and beyond, (Joyce's parents divorced when she graduated from high school) but thought she came to it through her husband Jimmy, not through her own heritage.

In Oklahoma City, Joyce worked fulltime and still completed her undergraduate education in three years. A master's degree and a Ph.D. in physiological psychology followed, also in three years, and then she received a postdoctoral fellowship. She worked as a sleep researcher, first with people and then with animals. When she moved to California, she studied people who lived under the flight pattern of 747's landing at LAX (she learned that their sleep physiology was quite disturbed), and did pain and stress management with burn patients. During this time, she was immersed in science, living a completely secular life in Laguna Beach, California.

Religion was not a part of her existence, yet she felt this gnawing ache that something was missing from her life. Constantly searching, she experimented by attending various churches, synagogues, lectures and yoga centers. One day Joyce stumbled on a lecture by Rabbi Jonathan Omerman, who was trained in Chasidic Judaism, a branch of Orthodox Judaism, and doing outreach for Jewish people who had left the fold. She felt like she had come home. Joyce started driving the two hours to Los Angeles every week to study with Omerman. Eventually she moved there to spend more time studying with him. He showed her a side of Judaism that was happy, festive, and spiritual. Although outwardly her life did not change much, internally she felt like a different person.

Fourteen years ago, Joyce moved back to Oklahoma City to take care of her aging mother. She found a job in a hospital rehabilitation department doing pain and stress management with the elderly. The essence of her existence, however, occurs after work. She studies the Torah several days a week with people from forty-five to ninety years old, attends lectures at Chabad, the center of the Chasidic movement in Orthodox Judaism, and the Jewish University, and has begun a three-year certificate program in Jewish end-of-life care to enrich her position as vice president of *Kvod v' Nichum*, the North American Jewish Burial Society. Surprised and thrilled to find so many Jewish opportunities in the "provinces" of Oklahoma, Joyce Kendall Friedman, at sixty-seven years of age, feels that she has arrived home: at a place that is familiar, comfortable and joyous. In her own words, she reflects on her religious quest and the long, winding path that brought her back to traditional Judaism, the Jewish community and a fulfilled spiritual core.

In her own words....

I have fond memories of spending weekends at my grandparents in New Jersey. It made me feel Jewish while I was there—lighting the candles, having a special dinner Friday night, spending time with them on Saturday—but once I went home, Judaism wasn't a part of my life. It was hit or miss until I met Rabbi Omerman, but I'm getting ahead of myself.

For most of my life, I was an academic, a scientist and a researcher. I looked very good on paper. For a while I was the world expert on genetics and sleep. My friends were brilliant and accomplished. One friend, an engineer, designed the system that sent the first photos back from the moon.

When I was a grad student, I was doing sleep research and did my dissertation on the genetics of sleep. I ran the animal sleep lab and implanted electrodes in hundreds of rats, mice and fish. Other people in my lab implanted them in alligators and in other animals. I stayed up all night to watch animals sleep, and made sure that the equipment functioned correctly.

I earned my Ph.D. in physiological psychology at age twenty-eight at the University of Florida and then received a postdoctoral fellowship in an electrophysiology lab at the University of Chicago. I had no time for spiritual stuff. I was working long days, looking at endocrine systems. It was all very mechanical: I was writing grant proposals to get funding; I did some teaching, but it was mostly research. My lab was in building 13, previously the morgue. I wore a white lab coat.

I didn't have time to deal with religion or spirituality. I was too busy.

While I was living in California, I owned eight different homes. I love old things, fixing them up and making them beautiful. So I'd move in, rehab the house and sell it. My favorite was a home in Laguna Beach overlooking the migrating whales and Catalina Island. I did a lot of forensic work: I was an expert witness in the area of survival from airplane crashes. Then I got sick with an autoimmune disease, which is in remission now. By then I had divorced twice. My second husband was a psychiatrist and molecular biologist. He was actually one of my residents but was the same age as me. He was interested in meditation and followed a California yogi to an ashram in the northwest.

After he left, I went back and got licensed as a clinical psychologist. I started seeing patients at the University of California at Irvine and was co-director of the outpatient clinic in the department of psychiatry. I was slowly oozing over to less science and more patient care.

My career was my life, but at the same time, there was a big empty space that wasn't filled. It's not like I wasn't doing useful things. At the University of California I was Chief of Mental Health Services at the UCI Burn Center for twenty years. My work made a difference, but my personal life was another story.

I started searching. I had friends who were Christians, so I went with them to the Methodist Church, and then I went with other friends to the Lutheran church for a while. Wherever my friends went, I followed. My mother took me to a Christian spiritualist church. We also went to a yoga center and meditated. When I was married, I'd go to Buddhist and yoga gatherings. Everyone sat on the floor, and we'd all mediate, and they'd burn incense. As an undergrad in the sixties, I did LSD looking for spiritual enlightenment. I thought at times I was getting close, but none of it was very happy. It was all very somber.

Then I heard about Rabbi Jonathan Omerman, whom Hillel, the campus organization for Jewish students, had hired to do outreach for wayward Jews. He was the guest speaker one night while I was living in Laguna Beach. I don't know why I went to hear him; something drew me.

I was very impressed–so impressed that I started driving to Los Angeles to study with him every week—two hours each way. He had studied Chasidism and showed me a side of Judaism that was happy. People sang and danced. It was exuberant, and it felt spiritual. Eventually, I moved to L.A., the city of angels, in my late forties to be closer to him and his teachings.

What made the difference when I met Rabbi Omerman was that people were finding joy in the world. People think being religious is a whole bunch of don'ts: don't eat that, don't do that on the Sabbath, and that the God of the Hebrew Bible is a vengeful God. That's not the God that I found. I found a loving God who's in the world, not removed from it, who wants us to find joy in the world.

I even started to go to rabbinical school. I wanted to learn more so I thought I'd become a conservative rabbi. But my Hebrew wasn't good enough, so I dropped out after a semester.

I spent huge amounts of time going to synagogue, being more observant, and studying the Torah. I did fewer and fewer secular things. I met a colleague, and he introduced me as "This is Joyce Friedman. She used to be scientist." Friends who were engineers and scientists thought I had run amok. They'd ask me, "How can you believe in something you can't see or measure?" It wasn't a problem for me. All the beauty in the world is evidence that there's a God, a prime mover. There has to be a God.

It's not that all of a sudden I was *Shomer Shabbos* (someone who strictly observes the commandments associated with the Sabbath). It wasn't a public thing...After my turning point, I don't know that the world would have noticed a difference. It was an internal one. I moved closer to my teachers and spent more time studying with them and studying on my own. My first two husbands were not Jewish; I could never marry a non-Jew again.

I felt more peaceful, and I had found a reason for being. I felt like I was needed for something. I wasn't floating around in the flotsam and jetsam of the world; I had a purpose here. Part of it now is to make sure people have a proper burial and a proper transition into the next life. That's my purpose now. They don't need to be embalmed with makeup and viewed.

Charity is important. I've refocused from material to spiritual. To learn what God wants for us, to repair the world here and now, so that God would want to be here. It's not a deferred gratification.

Now that I've moved back to Oklahoma City, it's hard to be Orthodox. I do attend Chasidic services at Chabad and study with Rabbi Goldman. Helene Harpman is my mentor here; she is a retired professor of Biblical Hebrew and Jewish Humor and Folklore at the University of Oklahoma. She teaches Torah and models how to live a proper Jewish life and how to do *mitzvoth* (good deeds). I keep kosher at home, but I do eat out—but only fish and veggies. On *Shabbos* (Sabbath) I try not to do what you're not supposed to do. But I have to drive to services; sometimes I need to work. I'm not rigid, but I'm doing the best I can.

I've been here fourteen years now; I'm really happy. I'm working at a Catholic hospital in rehab with people who've had strokes and hip replacements. I do pain and stress management and end-of-life care. I feel like I'm putting to use what I've come to be in the last years. It's really wonderful.

I do a lot with the Jewish Burial Society; that is a really important part of my life. Now I have to figure out a way to help more people understand what Jews do with end-of-life issues and how we can help each other. When you purify deceased people and dress them, they say, it's as if you're looking on the face of God. That's an amazing thought. The last thing to go after you die is your sense of hearing, so we talk to the deceased when we work with them; we assume they are capable of hearing. We do not pass things over them; their spirit hovers there. It's a truly amazing spiritual experience that they cannot thank you for. You're not doing it for anybody except the person who has died.

I still teach at Rose State Community College two days a week. I like teaching at a community college because people really want to learn. I always find a way to let them know I'm Jewish, in order to confront their stereotypes. I teach introduction to psychology and also human sexuality. I emphasize the brain and a lot of physiology in my classes. I try to point out the scientific beauty of how everything works. It's amazing that we can see at all because the visual system is upside down and backwards. How could that all be? Because God did a really good job!

My life is so different now. There are three things you're supposed to do as a religious Jew, and I'm doing more of each of them now: charity, studying Torah and prayer. I try to talk to God all the time. God is integral to everything; I have an ongoing conversation with Him.

I do all this study gladly, in addition to work, family and taking care of five rescued animals. I am so grateful that I am not a Jewish orphan in the Oklahoma buckle of the Bible belt. Who would have thought that so much Jewish community and learning was possible here?

I truly came home to myself when I stopped looking outside myself, beyond my heritage to fill the empty hole within my soul. I think we all have spiritual DNA, a plan for our lives that should not be denied. It's necessary to find the key to open the door so that we can get on with the plan. Now the only thing missing in my life is a Jewish husband to help complete my Jewish home.

Christine H. Johnson

On a Spiritual Journey

Today everyone talks about being on a spiritual path, which can mean everything from attending a yoga class once a week to going on solitary retreats in the mountains. For Christine Hedgley-Johnson, a retired R.N. whose spirituality is grounded in her Christian faith, the path has been long and deep. Along the way, she has garnered the tools to cope with life's many challenges.

As the daughter of an authoritarian Baptist minister, Christine grew up indoctrinated in Christian teachings. She and her twin brother David (he's seventeen minutes older) spent most of their youth challenging the old saying that a minister's kids are the "worst." They loved to get into mischief together, but didn't do anything really bad. They'd walk around during school activities arm and arm as though they were boyfriend and girlfriend, pretending to be lovey-dovey with each other. They didn't look like twins: He is six feet, three inches and dark and she is five feet, two inches and lighter. They also enjoyed pulling pranks, like removing their teacher's chair when she was ready to sit down. By today's standards their antics were innocent, but in those days, they created some havoc—especially for a minister's children.

Christine and David were born in Chicago, and at eight months of age, the family moved to Tallahassee where her father was chaplain and philosophy professor at Florida A & M University. They lived there until Christine was in third grade when her father received a pastorate in Winston-Salem, North Carolina. She spent the rest of her growing up years there.

It was not easy being this pastor's daughter. In fact, she lived in fear of him. He was a severe, demanding man who did not hesitate to whip his children. Her brother and father never got along. Even when David received a Ph.D. from Oxford, their father still treated him like "he didn't have a brain in his head." Unlike David, Christine learned not to push her father's buttons in an effort to get along.

Christine was closer to her mother, but at times she felt like a third wheel because her mother showered so much attention on David. He had some health problems, which required a mother's attention, and she wanted to make sure he kept his mind engaged so he didn't get into serious trouble.

Christine wanted to be a nurse, but her father told her nurses weren't respected and didn't make enough money; he refused to pay for a nursing education. He insisted she become a teacher and attend the college he graduated from; then he would help pay for her schooling. Christine complied with his wishes: She graduated from college and taught biology for one semester. Then she went to Lincoln School for Nurses and received a nursing diploma. After working as a nurse for a while, she received a scholarship to Boston University, where she received a master's in nursing.

In her early twenties (the turbulent 1960s), she joined the fight for civil rights for African Americans. This was a troubling time for her. She could not understand how God could let her people be treated with such disrespect, so she left the church. And thus started a spiritual journey that would last the rest of her lifetime.

In graduate school, she was very friendly with four army and navy nurses, who encouraged her to join the service. Upon graduation, she joined the U.S. Public Health Service Commission Corps (the medical arm of the Coast Guard) and was stationed on Staten Island, scheduled to start as a head nurse, but the chief nurse refused to supervise her because she was African American. Instead she was transferred to Baltimore where the climate was more accepting.

Christine was with the U.S. Public Health Service Commission Corps for twenty-three and a half years. She did not go out to sea but was stationed all over the United States: Maryland, California, Louisiana, Michigan, and New Mexico. She held mostly supervisory roles. She was fortunate to be transferred to New York where her husband worked for the New York Transit Authority; their two daughters were born there. They later divorced but remained friends. He died of a heart attack at age fifty-two in 1992.

She retired from the service in 1987 and taught at a community college for ten years, then left to do consulting work. Today she is very active in her Episcopal church, volunteers at a local shelter, and does ministry work in the state prison.

Like her mother and maternal grandmother, Christine gives informal counseling to whoever needs it. Everyone knows they'll get an honest response from her; she tells it like it is. They also know she likes to go out to lunch and for the price of a meal, she gives some pretty sound advice.

Although Christine never had an "aha moment" that changed her life dramatically like most of the women in this book, she experienced a number of significant turning points—her mother's death, giving up carousing, and surviving breast cancer—that, one by one, brought her back to the church and to her own spirituality. She has plumbed the darkest parts of her soul during the course of her spiritual journey, which has spanned her seventy-two years. Out of this deep knowing of her own self has come her acceptance and caring of others.

Among her friends, Christine is known for her willingness to listen, her receptivity and her kindness. One friend, who shares in the ministry of morning prayer and contemplative prayer with Christine at her church, said she feels like they're sisters, even though Christine is black and her friend is white. They also share North Carolina roots. "Chris always has an open heart and an open mind," her friend told me. Another friend, who exercises with her at the Community College gym and referred her to me, said, "She is an inspiring woman with a kind heart and a sharp mind. From the first time I met her in the locker room, I felt like we were kindred spirits."

As we'll see in the next section, Christine Johnson doesn't just talk the talk: she walks the walk.

In her own words....

I left the church because I was tired of being treated like a second-class citizen. It was the Sixties, and I was active in the civil rights movement: They refused to serve me at restaurants, I had to ride in the back of the bus—all that. They were hosing down Martin Luther King, Jr. My parents said, "It's to be expected. You have to pay your dues." I repeated, "I'm not a second-class citizen." I left the church because I didn't feel Jesus Christ was doing what He should. I had scholarships to go to school. I got a lot of accolades based on what I was doing in college and in my extracurricular activities. I figured, *I did that. God didn't do that. So I'm going to leave.* I was twenty-one years old.

My grandmother said she'd pray for me. My father said that I'd eventually return. He couldn't accept that I left the church, because he was a minister and what would people say?

I stayed away from 1957 until 1964. Then my mother got real sick—she had a stroke at fifty-three— and there was nothing I could do, even with a master's in nursing. She had led a great life; she had a master's in guidance from NYU, and she helped a lot of people. She still had her mind and she was still counseling people even though she couldn't talk. She'd be sitting at the kitchen table in her wheel chair, and you'd say something and she'd bang on the table and that made you think: What did I say? She would communicate through her nonverbal expressions.

When she passed five years later, I was a raving maniac and drunk! I was in my early thirties at the time. I regret to this day that she never knew my children.

She wanted to know that I had found my niche spiritually before she died. I didn't return to the Baptist church (She was Methodist and my father was Baptist), but I started visiting different churches while she was still alive. I was already in the Public Health Service, and I wanted to be able to go to church and have the same liturgy anywhere I was stationed. One Episcopal minister took a lot of time with me. I thought certain things came about because of what *I* did. He said, "No, this is not so; they are due to a Higher Being."

So slowly I eased back into going to church, and the next thing I knew, I became a youth sponsor. It was a turning point for me. I had been doing a whole lot of happy hours. I didn't have time to carouse and drink all night when I had to get up the next morning and do something with the scouts, a youth group or the church.

Coming back to church was part of coming home to my true self. When you work on your spirit, you have to come to grips with who you are—the darkest parts of you—to know that Jesus Christ is focused and well in your life. You don't make decisions without being open. You have to see the dark spots, or you don't move on. I chose to find my spirituality through a Higher Power and a church, but you don't have to go to church to be spiritual.

I became a whole different person: open, receiving, thoughtful and kind. I had every reason to lash out at other people, but I didn't. You learn not to respond to people who are hurtful. You turn away and pray for them. It keeps you grounded so when those things happen, you don't react. You have to work at not getting caught up in it. By not reacting, it diffuses things. I deal with issues that trouble me by walking in nature, mulling things over, and talking with the Higher Power.

Over time, I've developed this ability to stay calm. I used to be quite mouthy. I'm not like that any more. You can catch more bees with honey! I also have been told when people start talking, I just look at them and smile. I don't take my eyes off them. It makes them very uncomfortable. I say nothing. I just listen, and they keep talking.

This ability to not get rattled has developed as an outcome of taking time for self-reflection. If I'm under stress emotionally, there's a spiritual place I can go that helps me get over that stress. If I'm upset about something or something happens in my life—a major loss of a friend, in my case a husband, something with my children—then I have a place to go and I know that in time, I'm going to be okay with it. It may take a while to get there, but I know there's a place I can go.

For me, that place is my big blue and white recliner in my living room. I can sit there for hours. I look through the sliding glass doors onto the patio and watch the Sangre de Cristo Mountains. I need to have a focus. I like looking at something. Some people read. I focus on the mountains, and then things begin to fall into place. I take a cup of chai and just look, think, and read. It puts me in a good space. When I get up from that chair, I'm in a different place inside.

I don't sit there with any regularity but if something happens in my life that I feel I need that connection, then sitting becomes regular. It's there for me. I don't have to go anywhere. I don't have to tell anybody. I just get in that chair, and then I say, we gotta talk! When I walked into the house for the first time, I saw this spot and knew I'd buy the house.

Sometimes I sit before I'm going to meet someone who's looking for me to be there with her. I set the clock. Then I have time to regroup and get ready. I don't dress for the appointment before I sit. I can't get up and just grab my pocketbook and keys and walk out the door. I've learned that. I used to think I could change myself that quickly and be okay when I got to the person's house. But I found that I need more time to transition. I allow myself at least half an hour, forty-five minutes to come out of the phase of contemplation to check my messages, get dressed, then get to the person's house. That works for me now. It didn't work for me ten years ago.

I don't know if I can describe what happens when I sit in that chair. I take the time because I'm concerned about meeting with a person. I pray and ask for divine guidance. It humbles me that someone I know called me and asked me to have a cup of tea. I say, "What's this going to cost me?" I use humor a lot. "Is it a long one or a short one?" "I don't know," she'll say. "Well, let's go somewhere where we can talk, where they won't run us out," I'll suggest. Usually I'm humbled that someone would select me to unload on and put that amount of trust in me. It's heavy for me.

Two days later, I'll meet someone else and she'll say, "I hear you went to lunch with so-and-so. How can you stand her?" I say, "I did pretty good. She paid for the lunch." Everyone laughs. I don't have to say anything. Everyone knows I love to go out to eat, especially lunch. I'm on a fixed income. Lunch is cheaper than dinner. Lunch becomes my main meal for the day.

I learned this ritual of sitting and meditating when I went on religious retreat. The person who led the retreat was a female

Episcopal priest. (We're still friends.) I asked her, "You give so much: People come to you and you listen. How can you handle it?" She has a background in social work and counseling. She uses her background, plus what she learned in seminary. She pulls that all together. She helped me see myself as an individual, as a child of God, as a mother, and as a professional. She identified with all of those.

God has given me a sense of humor, and it has carried me through all my life. It diffuses things. That has saved me and saved many a relationship. You put things in a way that others can accept. That's better for me. Some people have hang-ups that they bring with them when they meet me. We have a race problem here even though there aren't that many African Americans. People who have moved here bring their prejudices. You can never relax.

The way I relate to people stems from my spirituality, from the inner peace it gives me. But I have to work on it all the time so I don't blow off the handle. I hope having met me and worked with me on boards, the prejudice will go down to fifty from one hundred. I try to find out more about the person so I don't judge the book by the cover. Open the book and see what's going on inside. There's always something. Even the worst person has something to give. You might have to dig to find it, but there's nobody made whose 100% bad. Something makes them come across that way.

So many experiences have made me who I am now. I never had an "aha moment." I have changed, though, like when I searched for a Higher Power when my mother got sick. Then I was stationed at different places, got married, and had children. I can be dense: God has to hit me with a two by four to get my attention. A couple of times I have been hit by a two by four, so that I moved where I needed to go: I learned certain things from my children, and I had to deal with my husband dying on the spot.

One daughter has never been right since her father died. He died on her birthday, and she blames everything on that. She's thirty-seven. He's been gone seventeen years, and she still asks me, "Mama, why'd he have to die on my birthday?" She hasn't come to grips with that. She has a long way to go.

In Proverbs 22:6, it says "Train up a child in the way he should go, even when he is old, he will not depart from it." My husband and I gave her a good upbringing. Hopefully, some day she'll go back and find those roots and decide what she wants to do with her life. I may have to wait a while for that. Now, I'm at the stage of saying to myself, please let her learn from this mistake. Let her get through this. Instead of her going eighty miles an hour, slow her down to fifty, then to thirty. Then she'll say, aha! That's what I did with my life: it took me awhile to get that moment. Someone was praying for me that would happen.

When I got cancer fourteen years ago, I would have had a really rough time if it weren't for my spiritual journey. It scared me to death. Mother had breast cancer, got over that, and then had the stroke. I got diagnosed at fifty-two. I thought: I'm going to be gone. But then I made up my mind. I'll just accept it; maybe my job here is done. Whatever it is, let me face it. If it's time to come to You, let it be. My twin brother came in, my best friend was there, and this community—they were all very good to me. They got me to my appointments, cooked my meals. It was one step at a time.

I didn't blame anybody. I was at peace. My faith gives me inner peace. Having had cancer and gone through it, I was able to help other people who were facing it, especially those who think it's a death sentence. It's not a death sentence. I was up and about. My youngest daughter bought me new clothes. I just accepted it and a lot more things came to me. People weren't afraid to sit with me. I was upbeat so everyone around me was too.

That cancer changed me. I'm very thankful for every day. Every morning I get up and say, "Thank you, Jesus." It makes you more attuned to people who are just getting a diagnosis. People will call me and say, "Chris, you're a nurse. Do you know anything about this?" I'll look it up for them. That's what I can do. I keep up with the latest nursing handbook. I don't have a lot of money. What am I supposed to do now that I'm not an active professional? I have fifty years of knowledge. What do I do with it? I want to use it and share it with others.

People say they want to know what it's like to have cancer. But they don't want the cake; they just want the frosting. There's nothing in whipped cream! Have substance to what you believe or the way you are. A wishy-washy person isn't good. Aging and the circumstances of your upbringing should have made you into a person of substance.

I heard this kind of talk from my grandmother when I was growing up. David and I spent several summers with her in Mississippi when my mother was getting her master's. My grandmother had an eighth grade education but had wisdom beyond a Ph.D. She was grounded in her faith and treated everybody like a first-class citizen. She carried herself like a first-class citizen even though she was a downstairs maid and a pastry cook. She dressed like she was going to university. No flies on her at all! She always looked people straight in the eye even though they treated her like a black woman. Yes, Miss Nettie had a reputation in town. She respected every human being, *every human being*. That's what my spirituality is about too.

When I sit in that chair and look at the mountains and thank God for putting me in this place at this time, it strengthens me and gives me sustenance for my spiritual journey. I call it a journey because you never arrive. God's working on you all the time. My Native American friends call It the Great Spirit. Before I was on this path, I was a pain in the ass. I really was. I had all this energy and hate before. I'm mischievous now, but I was really, really bad then. I got into anything I could possibly get into, had a couple of addictions. I was bad! But I had a mother and grandmother who prayed for me and saw something in me I didn't see.

I'm still working at coming home to my true self. I get a part of myself, and then something else happens. I back up and go another way. That's not too good either. It's a constant thing. I won't have arrived until they plant me!

For me, home is a comfortable place spiritually and emotionally. But I'm never home and *settled*. I may be home, I may be in a spot where I'm comfortable for three, six months, for a year, and then I realize that something else needs to be done with me as a person, so I can be a better mother, a better grandmother, a better Christian, a better friend. I don't see it as, "Well, I'm here now. I've arrived." There's always room for growth.

Elena Montano

Following the Steps Home

Coming Home

Elena Montano grew up poor in La Cienega, a small village south of Santa Fe in a home her grandfather homesteaded. Her father raised chickens but sometimes one of their neighbors would sneak in and steal them, along with the vegetables he grew, so they had to make do with even less. They lived on chili, beans, tortillas and potatoes for many years.

The oldest of nine children, Elena slept on a mattress with her two brothers until she got her periods and begged her mother to change the sleeping arrangements. Her family always called her by her English name, Helen, as they did all the children in the family, even though they only spoke Spanish at home. Her mother used her Spanish name only when she was angry with her. Then, it was, "ELENA!!!"

Elena couldn't wait to leave home when she graduated from high school so she joined the convent, determined not to repeat her mother's life. For the first time, she had enough to eat and was introduced to many new foods, like rhubarb. But the convent experience was short-lived: she left after eighteen months because of several bouts of stomach cramps and homesickness.

Unable to find work in New Mexico, her family moved to Southern California. There her father found construction work. Elena worked as a clerk in a five and dime store. There were still ten of them sleeping on mattresses on the floor, but they had better food. For the first time in her life, Elena tasted pizza and burritos, and she liked them.

Elena married the first man who asked her out. He was a nice, quiet Italian guy. Even though he was not Hispanic, her family liked him because he was Catholic; Elena also had an aunt who was half Italian, so that made him more acceptable. She got pregnant right away and had two more daughters within five years. Their marriage came apart when her youngest was three years old. He told her he had fallen out of love with her and was going to leave. He threatened to leave for six years before he actually did.

With her marriage on the rocks, Elena used food to comfort herself and gained a lot of weight. She went to a twelve-step program for about a year, but when her husband left, she lost her motivation to lose weight and let herself go.

To support herself and her three daughters, she opened a day care center in her home, which she operated on a shoestring and became very successful. She felt proud of her self-sufficiency, took her ex-husband to court for child support, and had money in the bank for the first time in her life. Despite these achievements, she was plagued by compulsive overeating and an addiction to sugar. Once she ate something sweet, she lost all self-control.

Not only did Elena gain considerable weight, but she lived in fear. She was sarcastic and angry much of the time. She blamed everyone else for her problems, yet inside she felt she was not good enough or thin enough or tall enough. She knew she was miserable and stuck, but didn't know what to do about it.

In 1988, she moved back to New Mexico and into the house in which she grew up. Her father had passed away and her mother, who was a semi-invalid, died two years later. After the death of her parents, she didn't know what to do, so she decided to meet with a counselor. After that meeting, she realized she had to make some changes and did two things that transformed her life. She earned a college degree, and she went back to the twelve-step program and approached it as a spiritual practice. Although her addiction was not to drugs or alcohol, food had the same grip on her life. Through working the program, following the steps and consulting with her sponsor daily, Elena at seventy feels like she finally has her inner home in order. She is proud of herself: a self that is lovable, teachable and filled with gratitude.

In her own words....

Growing up, I'd see my mom cry because there wasn't enough food. We had very little clothes, mostly hand-me-downs. I'd wear boys' pants. We'd bathe once a week, on Saturday. We slept three in a bed. We weren't allowed to speak English, and we didn't celebrate birthdays. My father would spank us on our birthdays. He thought this was funny; now I think it was cruel. My first birthday celebration was when I was nineteen years old in the convent.

I went to the convent because I wanted to leave home. We weren't told that we could go to college. You could be a nurse or secretary but no higher than that. We had to finish high school, and then we were expected to get married and have kids. I refused to go through what my mother went through, so I went to the convent. That brought fame to the family. Wow! It was like we have a nun in the family. What I liked best was that I got enough to eat. Of course, I gained some weight. When I left the convent, we moved to California because there were no jobs here; I was making eighty cents an hour at the hospital.

I met my husband in California at the store where I was working. After I got married, I get pregnant right away—very Catholic! Our marriage started failing after a few years. He said he didn't love me anymore and he'd be leaving me. My mom used to say the same thing when we were too noisy: "I'm going to leave you" and she'd start packing her bag. It scared us. That stayed with me. When he said that, I was scared too. He did that for six years. He'd say, "I'll paint the room now because by next summer I'll be gone." We rarely had sex. They stopped giving me birth control, so we didn't have sex. I wanted it but he didn't. It was always on his time.

I went to the twelve-step program for a year, because I'd put on a lot of weight. (I had to eat sweets in the bathroom because he didn't like fat women.) During that time, I started standing up to him. I told him he couldn't talk to me like that anymore, and so he left. It was very hard for me. I never asked my family for money, but I got a lot of help from my church. I had a big day care center in my home. My girls would help me. I took the kids to anything that was free: the zoo, swimming pools.

Once he left, I didn't care about me. I thought, I'm ugly, I'm not enough, so I might as well be fat. I'd have twelve kids for breakfast. I'd eat their leftovers, then I'd have my breakfast. At ten a.m. I'd have a sandwich, because I feared I'd lose my energy. At noon, I'd eat their leftovers from lunch. When they napped, I'd have my own lunch. Parents would send nice snacks, and I'd give the kids peanut butter and jelly, and I'd eat the good snacks. At dinner, my girls would say, "Here's my plate, Mom," and I'd eat their leftovers. At night, I'd get a big box of Cheerios and eat half of it or scoop rocky road ice cream from the carton. It was an addiction.

When I hit one hundred-sixty-five pounds, I stopped weighing myself. It wasn't that I just gained a lot of weight. It was my attitude: I felt like I was going crazy. I was nasty with people. I didn't care; I had no guilt. I didn't care who I hurt. I'd never admit my faults. I lived in fear of the "what if's." I didn't know how to hug—I had a lot of body shame— or to say, "I love you" to myself or to anyone. I was quick with anger and had a cussing tongue. I didn't know how to laugh; I was always serious. I was very religious with no spirituality. I didn't know I had feelings. I was a good actress and showed the world how great I was; yet inside I hated myself.

I just knew I had to do something different, so I went back to the twelve-step program. I became serious about it and did every thing that I could to help myself: I went to workshops and retreats, and I started walking. I was angry all the time, so I'd run, and then I'd walk to get rid of my anger. I learned how to write Dear God letters and how to journal. I still do it every morning. I learned how to pre-plan my food, which helps me maintain my weight loss.

In the program, we discuss changing self-talk: Accepting me as I am and accepting others as they are. Hearing other people share their own stories, I learn a lot, and I get self-help messages from them. I needed to learn to sip life rather than guzzle it. I get a lot of support from the people in the meetings, and I also learn from the ones who aren't doing so well because it reminds where I came from. I used to blame the world. Now I look within myself. I have a lot of gratitude. I'm aware of my own faults. I don't like the fourth step, which is about making a searching and fearless moral inventory of ourselves, but if my sponsor tells me to do it, I'll do it.

I lost over forty pounds, and I've maintained my weight loss. I know now that I'm allergic to sugar. When I eat it, I have intense cravings for food, all foods. And the next day, I always want more. Food is a mood-alterer; I get very emotional and can't think straight.

I still have this craving to eat at three p.m. I know it's emotional, so I make phone calls or write Dear God letters. I ask Him to guide me in what I'm supposed to do. Or I'll tell Him, I don't feel like doing this, I want to read my novel. What should I do? Writing it out helps.

It was hard for my family to know that I didn't eat sugar, but now they respect me. They look at me like I'm on a diet. I don't care how they see it as long as they appreciate me. I work with my sponsor. On the holidays, I thought I could have a little bit of sugar, but I don't know what the hell a little bit is. Now, what I do is call my sponsor and commit myself for today to not eat sugar; or when I get close to my family's home, I call her again and tell her I'll commit not to eat anything that I'm not supposed to. Once I call my sponsor, the craving leaves. If I don't call her, I'll eat a whole bag of potato chips easily.

When I came back from California, my mother was still alive. We had never been close, but at the end we became friends. Three days before she died, she said, "I love you." I never heard those words from her before. When I was eight years old, I wanted to give my mom a hug, and she said I was too old for that. I was always too old or too fat or too short, all that stuff. It left me with never feeling that I had or was enough. It was very painful for me. I vowed I'd never hug my mom again, and I didn't.

After my mom died, I went to a counselor and told him I didn't know what to do with myself. He knew I was going to a twelve-step program, so he said I could be a substance abuse counselor. That sounded cool, and I could get financial aid. I took three classes for the program and three classes that I wanted. I took a lot of psych and a lot of English. It was great.

One of the classes I took was on grief. We were encouraged to complete unfinished business. I was always known as Helen, but I had received a Spanish name at baptism, and I wanted to get it back. I felt I needed to do this. I no longer wanted my husband's name, Botacchi or my English name, Helen. In 1994, I became Elena and took back my maiden name, Montano. My family still calls me Helen. At first I corrected them, but then I felt that it really doesn't matter. I don't care what they call me anymore. The important thing is I feel complete now. This is who I am.

I really enjoyed the classes and graduated from college with honors at age fifty-eight. I was a substance abuse counselor for five years. Then I worked in a teenage boys' recovery center, but they were dangerous; I didn't like that. I worked as a substitute teacher for a while, then at Wal-Mart and in a soup kitchen. I also do a lot of charity work. I pick up food from the bakeries and supermarkets and take it to the shelters.

I did other things that I never thought I could do. I took swimming lessons—I never knew how to swim. I took dancing lessons. I never liked to dance because I had such body shame, such low self-esteem about my body. That helped me accept my body as it is. That was the hardest thing I ever did. The classes helped an awful lot. I even went to Toastmasters in English and in Spanish. I can be a comedian!

It's funny—When I was forty and my ex was leaving, I felt so ugly and old and terrible. Today at seventy, I feel younger. I love myself, I take care of me. I never used to accept my height; I'd wear those high heels. I used to be four feet, eleven. I'm four feet, eight now. I like me as I am. I laugh more, I joke more. I was so serious while I was raising the kids, because I was scared all the time.

Anger rarely comes any more. I think it out, then write it out. The journal writing and recording my food every day helps a lot. I share a lot at meetings and go to them three times a week. I take care of an elderly person three times a week too. I take my own pre-planned food with me, and I cook healthy meals for her.

I'm dating a guy seven years older than me. Never say never! I met him at Wal-Mart's; he's a greeter. Sex with my ex was wham, bam, thank you, ma'am. Once I timed it and it was three minutes, and then he'd push me away like I was a piece of furniture. This guy is different. Oh, my God. We didn't have sex for the first three months we dated. We went to Albuquerque for a show, and he said we'd stay over night because it would be too dark to drive back. Yeah, right! I bought this red nightgown. We had sex so many times that night. Wow! And he never pushes me away. I feel like a twenty-year-old.

He's very knowledgeable about New Mexico history. That's not my interest. My interest is in what my day is like today, what I can do to take care of myself, and what is the next right thing to do. I keep it basic. Sometimes the next right thing to do is to rest or go for a walk.

He loves history and sports. I'm a runner, a mover. I always have a project going. I like to stay busy. We've been together three years. We each live in our own houses, and we date and travel together. We're good companions. Our living situation works well for us. We're not ready to get married yet. What's different is that I accept him for who he is. I don't try to change him. That's a turnaround for me: accepting other people. In the past, I had no qualms about telling people what I felt. I'd tell them, "I don't like this in you." I felt I *had* to tell them. Now I have acquired a healthy guilt. I will stop and think before I speak, or I'll apologize.

These changes began when I started becoming serious about taking better care of myself (when I weighed one hundred-sixty-five pounds). It's a process; it's not perfect. You take two steps forward and one step back. It's progressive and you keep going uphill.

I'm more serene now. I don't like the word happy; it's a short-lived feeling. I don't have fears anymore. I used to be so fearful of everything. I lived in the "what ifs" and "if only's." I don't do that any more. In accepting myself, I can accept others as they are. When I was in the day care business, parents would come in and I couldn't stand up to them to tell them they needed to pay me for overtime. Someone told me to sit the parent down while I stood up. That felt so good. It gave me self-worth and confidence.

There are a lot of things I don't know, and I don't have the need to know about everything any more. I know my boundaries, like I catch myself before I gossip. I see a lot of changes in myself. The biggest change is in my self–love and self worth.

I needed new shoes for church. I've always had hand-me-downs or clothes from a thrift shop. I decided I'm going to buy me brand new shoes. I'm better than that. I deserve a pair of new shoes. I'm not one who needs too much, but that felt good.

Coming home to myself is truly knowing myself and loving myself; how others think of me does not concern me. I work at keeping my inner home in order. I'm comfortable with me, with what I have and don't have. I no longer compare myself to others or wish to have what others have. I know that I am human and seek help when I need it. I am pleased with my life as it is and grateful for my mind, body and spirit. I am enough.

Sharon J. Montgomery

Recovering Her Lost Childhood

Coming Home

Sharon J. Montgomery was the "war baby" of a sixteen-year-old mother and an Air Force father, who was stationed in India during World War II. He returned from the war when she was two. She was excited to finally see him but as she got older, her mother tried to keep her away from him— fearing that Sharon would reveal her mother's secrets if they got too close. Sharon grew up thinking her father didn't love her, but that was not the case: her mother had kept him from her because Sharon talked so much.

When she was young, her parents drank and never went to church, but would drop Sharon and her sister off at the Baptist church for Sunday School. Sharon was baptized at thirteen but didn't understand the ritual or feel at all moved by the ceremony. After she took her father to a tent revival where he was saved, the whole family began attending the Methodist church and did so until she graduated from high school. From a young age, she loved to draw, but since her parents thought it was a useless pastime and there was no extra money, she wasn't allowed to own a paintbrush while she lived at home.

Sharon had little memory of the first thirteen years of her life. She was close to her younger brother but she and her sister slept together in a baby bed until she was in the second grade, so they fought all the time. She remembers that her father, an electrician who was a self-made man, was angry and often verbally abusive to her. Her mother, also a victim of his abuse, did not defend Sharon. All Sharon knew was that she wanted to get out of the house. That coincided with her parents' plan for her: They told her she had to leave home at eighteen or start paying rent. There was no money for college if you were a girl, and she didn't feel smart enough to attend anyway because she couldn't spell and was dyslexic, so she started looking for a husband.

At nineteen, she met a handsome army lieutenant at her best friend's wedding and six months later, they were walking down the aisle. Although she was sexually attracted to him, her main motivation to get married was so she could leave home.

After six weeks of marriage, her husband was shipped off to Korea. Ironically, she rented the upstairs bedroom from her parents and worked for a dentist while he was away. When he returned, they moved to Chicago, where their first son was born. Over the next twenty years, he had tours in Vietnam and Germany. They had another son and a daughter. There were good times in their twenty-eight-year marriage, but the artist and the lieutenant colonel were never very compatible.

At each of their different locations, Sharon went to college to educate herself as an artist. She studied print making and painting and became a master printer; because of the quality of her portfolio, she was allowed to take graduate courses at three different universities. As she became more immersed in her work as an artist, her roles as artist and military wife began to clash. She could play the role of colonel's wife (he had moved up) when necessary, but he felt threatened by her talent; when she had an art opening, he would attend but to truly support her artistic career was out of the question.

After his twenty-year anniversary with the army, her husband left the military and took his first civilian job in Indiana. Sharon attended Indiana State University, then after three years they ended up in Edmond, a small town just north of Oklahoma City. She immediately opened her first art studio in the historical Paseo Arts District of Oklahoma City and began teaching print making.

Living together full-time for the first time in twenty years, intimacy issues arose. They both had affairs. He refused to go to marriage counseling, so she paid for a year of psychotherapy for herself by bartering with her artwork. At the end of that period, she knew it was time for her to move on. Her children were in a good place: One son was married, the other two were in college.

Now it was time to take care of herself. She divorced her husband and told me in an interview, "I left Oklahoma to birth myself."

Throughout the first forty-five years of her life, Sharon felt restless, like there was a big wound, an empty, festering hole that needed to be filled. She knew there was a part of her life that she didn't understand, but didn't have the courage to explore it. Her continued lack of connection to her parents' new Church of God propelled her to begin searching for spiritual meaning in her own life. One way she did this was to begin meditating. She started in 1988 in Oklahoma—this was the beginning of her search for the truth—and continues to meditate every day.

The next year, newly divorced, Sharon headed to New Mexico. A gallery on Santa Fe's illustrious Canyon Road had commissioned her artwork, and she also knew she'd find support for her new spiritual interest in meditation. As the significance of meditation grew and she met alternative healers, she began to search for the blank spots in the first thirteen years of her life. Because she had no medical insurance, she had not seen a medical doctor in years although she had worked with psychotherapists. Becoming more spiritually focused, she preferred working with alternative healers who she trusted, feeling they were on the same wavelength.

In her own words, Sharon tells of her experiences with healers, with uncovering her early childhood sexual abuse, and with coming to terms with her history. Processing this information has resulted in a profound transformation: She now knows herself in the deepest sense of the word and her art has flourished and shifted into new directions. Today she is a successful, widely exhibited artist in Oklahoma who creates ceramics, mixed media assemblages and works in glass and porcelain. At sixty-five years of age, Sharon J. Montgomery feels whole for the first time in her life.

In her own words....

When I came to New Mexico I had no memory of the first thirteen years of my life. I had always blamed my first husband for being emotionally unavailable, but when I looked at myself, I realized that I needed to explore why my emotions weren't available either. Up until that time, I didn't have the courage or spiritual base to look at those years.

Initially, I chose to work with alternative healers because I didn't have medical insurance. When I was in Oklahoma I had a physician who wanted to remove my female organs because I was bleeding. That's when I went to my first healer, who worked with me to stop the hemorrhaging. I still have all my organs today. The lack of medical insurance for twenty years and the choice of alternative healers to clear and support my emotional body has been a gift.

I decided to go to a meditation center when I arrived in Santa Fe. Someone there gave me a referral for Norman, a craniosacral therapist and hypnotherapist. I told him about the memory loss from my childhood and that I felt I was sabotaging my own success. I liked working with him, because I remained dressed; that was important for me with a male therapist. Craniosacral work reveals memory and moves energy to release the body's flow. He started that work and then suggested I work with Liz, who does past life regressions.

I spent ten years going back and forth to different healers depending on how vulnerable I was at the time. Initially, I didn't know what my memories were. Liz encouraged me to relax using exercises that were taking me into my body. I remember being panicked at first, so I went slowly and received deep spiritual support that protected me and allowed me to enter my own early life.

While on her table, I had a flashback of the playground where I attended Catholic school in south Texas. I was in the first grade and could smell a squashed pear and saw my lunch sack with a wet spot on it; I was carrying the brown paper bag. I remember going inside a big door where there was a small chapel. Next to the chapel there was a music room. Something happened to me in this room. Somehow I accidentally broke my inkwell. A nun slapped my hands with a ruler, and I became hysterical. I said to Liz, "Get me away from her" and jumped off the table. This nun frightened me, so I didn't want to stay with the regression.

In the second regression, I went back to the playground and on leaving the playground I went into the small chapel. The next time I went in there I saw a little girl on the altar on her knees with a priest and saw the oral sex. I didn't know it was me. The girl looked exactly like me, but I was standing outside of my body. I didn't connect what I saw to myself.

Later, I got a headache and asked Liz for a Tylenol. When I put the pill in my mouth, I choked and spit it across the room. I said, "Oh, my God, now I know why I could never swallow a pill. It *was* me." I retrieved the memory; it came back completely. First I witnessed someone else and then I understood that it was me. I remembered that the nun who hit me with a ruler had taken me to the priest; this nun was not my homeroom teacher. In the first regression my body could handle only so much. The second session revealed the rest of the truth. In 2009 I actually called the convent and had them send me pictures of several rooms, so my visions in the regressions were true.

When the memory came back, I started laughing and then crying. In the beginning I thought it was something that I had witnessed; I couldn't believe it was me. I have chosen not to do more regressions to learn if the abuse happened more than once.

I went back to Norman, the craniosacral therapist, and told him, "I'm so angry. I need to talk to this son of a bitch." He hypnotized me, but I didn't think the hypnosis was working, because I could hear his voice clearly. He took me down a set of stairs. I took two friends with me for support. At the bottom, the priest was sitting at a table. There were men on both sides of him. I remember screaming at him: "Go away! Get out of my life!" I called him every name in book. All of a sudden there was stillness. Then the priest spoke to me and said, "You can't just throw me away. You used me for what you want in this lifetime." This made me calm. That's when I knew I had been hypnotized.

I didn't tell anyone what the priest said. The next morning in my meditation, I saw the priest again. I told him: "I hate you so much, my rage is enormous. Not only are you destroying my life, but you're destroying the lives of other children!" I ended my tirade with the understanding that I had found my own spiritual life because of this painful experience. That day I could forgive him. That was a huge gift.

My determination to heal myself was profound. After continuing to do therapeutic work for a decade in several other modalities, I came to the final part of my healing.

Through friends, I had met Medicine Bear, a Lakota Sioux medicine man and did a Native American sweat ceremony with him. In the sweat lodge he told me I needed to make a burial ceremony for the men in my life who had hurt me. He said, "I had to bury my own father more than once in this ritual, and he is still alive." He advised me to make a clay figure of the priest and my grandfather, who I had discovered had also abused me. I had never worked in clay before; I had only done paintings and etchings, but I made the figures out of clay and we did the burial. They were my first figures in clay, my very first terracotta sculptures. Making them in clay allowed me to witness what had happened to me, and then more visions returned. I made them look real, showing the priest's robe and his penis. When I made the girl doll (like Sparkle Plenty from the Dick Tracy comic strip), I knew I was making my own self as a child.

My artwork changed completely after the burial. I started doing sculpture. In fact, I went back to school to study sculpture and started doing three-dimensional art at Arizona State University. Heading south I went to Baja, Mexico to work in bronze but never had enough money to do it. I loved working with the bright colors of Mexico and my artwork became completely abstract—after thirty years of being a realistic painter. Many of these new pieces grew out of the healing sessions.

The art I'm producing now is created from my inner child, who is no longer wounded. One of my dreams is to produce a sculpture for my old Catholic school. At this moment I'm happy working with colors, but I feel I'll change again as an artist. I'm writing a lot too. Many artists work in more than one medium. I go back and forth with three different media—two-dimensional, three-dimensional and writing. It's the way I prefer to work, and I've produced some of my best works of art and writing at this stage of my life.

My healing allowed me to honor who I really am. Until that time I was taking on everyone else's personality. That's what happens when you're abused. When you're robbed of your identity as a child, you don't know who you are. I've been lucky to be in the right place at the right time. Synchronicity is tremendous. I'm aware of a lot of things that people don't pay attention to. All my life, this road that I traveled has proved a blessing. If I didn't understand the ramifications of karma, I couldn't say that.

During the time I dealt with the abuse by the priest, I married a man from Punjab, India. I learned at the end it was a green card marriage, but the exchange was perfect because his children lived with an abusive mother in India, and I adopted them and brought them to America. We later divorced because of the pressures from his Indian family, and he has since died. He was the Sikh warrior who stood beside me when I had no emotional support from my birth family. This marriage occurred during the six most important years of my sensitive work to recover my lost childhood. Although our marriage ended with a financial loss for me, gaining my sanity and removing his children from the dirt floors of India made it all worthwhile. I am still close to his daughter and son. We both had mothers who lied to us, so we're very much alike.

After the memories came back, I looked at my parents differently. I know now that my grandfather beat my mother (his only child) when he was drinking. Although she has chosen not to honor the secrets I've uncovered, I understand why. In my relationship with my father, I had always thought there was something unspoken, but now I know he was not the man who hurt me, that he did love me after all. Late in life I learned to forgive my parents, because I realized I couldn't ask them to give me what they didn't have to give.

The burial ceremony was a powerful turning point for me. It freed me emotionally and also gave me freedom with my art. It takes time on this journey for the understandings of the mind to penetrate the marrow of the bones. Gradually, after extensive healing therapies and daily meditation, my energy is much calmer when I deal with everyday life. I'm still an artist excited about life but I operate from a healthier place. My new spiritual base has given me courage to trust my judgments and choices in relationships.

I'm at the best part of my life now. I've walked through all the pain. I'm grateful that I had the courage to do this healing work. I'm also more willing to put my story on the table. I know it's heavy; I wish it were lighter but it isn't. I feel strongly that it's important to be heard and not stifle my own voice, which I did for many years. I learned a long time ago that chaos would always be here, so meditation elevates my consciousness and helps prioritize my life.

At sixty-five, I'm much freer, and I would not be a day younger. I have learned to be content with me, but I still work constantly to change my self-talk. Even though I'm a people person, I'm comfortable spending time alone and value each moment of every day. I am slowly observing beauty—to feed the birds and feel the wind. My heart is much more grateful for these small things. Gratitude can take me out of a lonely moment.

I realized a long time ago I am responsible for my own happiness. I can't change other people, but I can change myself: I can alter how I view the world by praying for truth, and I can learn to understand pain and grow from it in order to transform myself.

The most important thing I have learned is that I am not separate from God; my Christian upbringing separated me from Him. Ironically, it was the priest who brought me back to God, a big lesson in forgiveness. Inside the dark is light and some kind of spiritual base always provides an important foundation. Life never stops flowing, and it cannot be rushed.

I know when you speak the truth someone hears you. All I do is plant seeds and have no expectation to when someone waters them. Just one person collecting knowledge moves the mountain of any family. I have watched my family's reaction to my changes; even if they don't understand, they notice. My younger sister, my brother and I all are finally closer. The most important thing is to change the negative flow inside your own self.

A guru once told me the work you do affects your family seven generations before you and seven generations after you. This knowledge makes my work possible. So I am paddling as fast as I can, for the generations of my grandchildren are looking me in the face.

Bea Duran-Tioux

Connecting to her Ancestors' Spirit

Coming Home

Bea Duran-Tioux's family has lived in the Tesuque Pueblo, north of Santa Fe, since the 1300s. She and her two brothers and four sisters grew up in her grandparents' sprawling adobe house. She remembers that they didn't have much furniture, so there was plenty of room for them all to gather around the fireplace and listen to their grandfather tell stories. Without a radio or television, storytelling was their evening entertainment.

Bea grew up with clay because her mother was a potter. She would often sit with her mother and make pots or animal figures, but as a child, she didn't like the things she made or enjoy the feel of clay on her fingers. Her father, a student of Dorothy Dunn's (a renowned art instructor at the Santa Fe Indian School), was a painter and print maker. He'd enlist his kids to paint with watercolor on the hundreds of three-inch bowls her mother had made, which they then sold. Bea did it grudgingly; she wanted to be outside playing.

When she was nine, she met an old Hopi man who was selling traditional ceremonial clothing, which he had made and embroidered, and something resonated with her. From that moment on, she knew that she wanted to be *that* kind of an artist when she grew up. But it was a long, circuitous path for her to get there. The beginnings and endings of her three marriages helped define her journey, but the underlying theme of her life has been the pursuit of her craftwork. This work is not simply a vehicle for self-expression. It has a much deeper meaning for her: it is a way to connect with her ancestors.

A rebellious high school student, Bea couldn't wait to get off the reservation, so when she graduated, she became part of a relocation program sponsored by the Bureau of Indian Affairs. They relocated her to Los Angeles, where she went to business school, because her father had talked of opening a business. She knew that many natives couldn't take the city life and had to return to the reservation, but she was determined to stay in the big city. She met her first husband there, who was non-native, and they had two children together. They were happy for a few years, until he got into drugs and alcohol. After eleven years, she left him and took her children back to Tesuque.

At home, she struggled with the tribal government, trying to buy land and a house and to receive financial aid. She eventually landed a job in a gift shop, but that was short-lived, as they wanted her to work for very little pay.

When someone from the Institute of American Indian Arts (IAIA) offered her a scholarship to learn museum training, she jumped at the chance. Although she never used her skills in a museum, they were helpful when she opened her own gallery on the reservation. At IAIA she met her second husband, a woodworker who had his own business, and they had three girls. With her husband's support, she was able to stay home and do the embroidery and weaving that she loved. She also ventured into pottery and drum making. They had many good years together, traveling to craft fairs to sell their work and seeing much of the country, Mexico and Canada.

But after twenty years together, he told her he didn't want to be married any longer. Devastated, she fought the divorce initially but after a year, she consented. Then she had to go to work fulltime to support her growing family. Another marriage to a native from Isleta Pueblo ended with his death after they were together for ten years.

The ending of each marriage represented a turning point for Bea, because she felt so dependent on her husbands. With them gone, she had to reconsider her life anew: What did she really want to do now? How could she make a living and still satisfy her soul? Who was she without a husband? She was overwhelmed after each marriage dissolved, but in time, gathered her strength and her resources to move on. And every time, she returned to the same personal home: the embroidery and weaving of her ancestors.

Today Bea Duran-Tioux supports herself as a seamstress at a hat store. It's just a job; her real work is her craftwork, which she sells every August at the Santa Fe American Indian Market (SWAIA), the largest of its kind in the country, and works on commissions during the year. This work is a spiritual path for Bea: a way to embody her heritage, connect with her ancestors, and pass on her rich history to her five children and fifteen grandchildren. As she explains in her own words, doing this work has brought her home to her deepest self at sixty-two years of age.

In her own words....

I was the middle child of six kids, so I guess I had the middle child syndrome. There were times I felt like I didn't belong, not being the oldest or the youngest. There were cousins around all the time too, yet it seems like I was always alone. I wasn't lonely but I felt alone. I spent a lot of time with my grandmother. We'd take the ashes from the fireplace and stove down to the ash pit in the *arroyo* or gather herbs or collect wood for the fire. We were always walking, and she was always talking to me. Not stories—just talking about whatever came up at the time. I learned so much from her, especially about herbs and dyes, and about herself as a child, and just about everyday things. This is when I was three or four years old.

When I got older, nine or ten, we'd hang around my uncle who is about the same age as we are. His father, our grandfather, would take us to his field in the horse-pulled wagon. We'd help him pull weeds and then we'd play the rest of the day; in the evening he'd tell us stories. Sometimes two or three of us would braid his long hair while he was resting on a chair. He'd laugh when he'd see his hair in the mirror.

One day my grandmother, my father's mother, took me to visit her brother, who lived nearby, when he was in his eighties or nineties. It was a nice sunny day. He only lived a block and a half away but it seemed to me like we walked for miles and miles. I was very young, but I remember there was a wall on the left and a fireplace and an earthen floor. When my eyes adjusted to the darkness, I saw an old man sitting on the floor on a sheepskin rug; the only light in the room came from a skylight. He was weaving a traditional red belt on a back strap loom. That stayed in my mind because he was the first and last person I saw weaving in my village.

When I was nine, this Hopi man, a friend of the family, came to our home. I remember this like it happened yesterday. He had a gunnysack and turned it upside down and shook it. Everything fell out onto the floor. I felt like wow! Those colors just jumped at me—like a rainbow. There were sashes, and kilts and belts that he had made, traditional clothing that our people wear when we're dancing. When I saw all those colors and designs I knew then that's what I wanted to do when I grew up. It was such a feeling; it took me back a hundred years and made me think about my ancestors. But then, I'm always thinking about them.

Just for a second, I wondered, who's going to teach me? But it didn't matter at that point. I just knew it was something I had to do. I couldn't find the words to express what I felt, but the colors and the designs danced at me as if the spirits had sent a sign or a message to me. There was actually no one in my family to teach me, but my mother laid some of the ceremonial clothing on the table so I could study them to see how they were made. I don't know if anybody today wears clothing they made themselves. I know people were buying traditional clothing from a few people who made kilts, sashes, moccasins and belts, but now they tend to make more ceremonial clothing.

My mother kept the very first belt I wove on a simple beading loom. She gave it back to me when I came home from California, and then I gave her one of the first belts I wove after I set up my loom with the heddle and shuttle.

I didn't have an instructor or mentor when I started to weave. I did research in libraries and in museums, but the challenge was when I actually did the work. I spent many hours at the loom, and weeks and even months went by while I figured out how to set up the warp with the shuttle and heddle, and learned how to form designs.

The same thing happened when I tried to make drums. There was no one to teach me, so I taught myself. With aching muscles, cuts and bruises, I eventually mastered my own techniques. By the late eighties and nineties, I was teaching drum-making at the Pueblo of Pojoaque.

All this craftwork fascinated me but I also wanted to be an anthropologist. As I said, I was always thinking about my ancestors. Always finding arrowheads and pottery shards. When I'm walking, I find this or that; I keep everything that I find. When I was in high school, I was taking evening classes in anthropology. I wanted to continue my studies after high school, but my father told me I couldn't study my own people—digging up their graves and writing about them. He said I'd probably be good at it, but it's against our beliefs and there would be consequences to pay—punishment by the spiritual beings. Disappointed, I had to change my education plan, but I never lost interest in the history of my people. It just took another form. It shows in my work and when I teach my children and grandchildren our written and oral history.

When I went to Los Angeles in the late Sixties after high school, I survived because I knew who I was, where I came from, and where I wanted to go. There were a lot of people who left the res and went to the big city and didn't make it; they couldn't take the white man's world. I'm a determined person; I decided I'd stay and make it there for a while. The school found me a job working part-time for the Firestone Tire Company; I was making good money and going to classes. Then I got married, and we moved. I'd find odd jobs wherever I went and got along with everybody. It was hard: going to the big city, not really knowing people, being alone, getting on the bus or train; but I knew I could do it, and I did.

I know my parents worried that I'd get into the drug and alcohol scene. My father always told us to put a limit on everything we do; that's what I tell my children, and I hope that our ancestors serve them in the same way that they serve me, because I never forgot them.

There were times I missed home and my family and friends. I didn't really like big city living, but I had made a commitment to myself to stay just to prove to myself that I could. If I travel now, I want to visit museums and the native people who live there. The big cities—seen one, seen them all. There was a time when we talked about going to Belize; I wanted to rent a hut on the beach and lie in a hammock and go into the jungle. I didn't want to stay in a hotel.

No matter what was happening in my life, it was always my embroidery work and the weaving that connected me to my ancestors and that brought me home to myself. Making drums had the same effect. For our people, the drum is the heartbeat of all living things. When our people migrated, they became tired, hungry and sick; the beat of the drum revived them so they could sing and dance again and continue on their journey.

Actually for me, everything is connected to my ancestors. I always wanted to know more, especially about the oral history, the stories. I was always asking questions. My mother taught me a lot, and I read a lot of books. Going to other villages I heard stories too, which are interesting. From learning our people's history and my family's past, I gained strength and knowledge about myself.

When my second husband decided he didn't want to be married to me any more, I didn't know what to do. I was so dependent on him. I wondered, how will I survive? I knew I *would* survive, but I felt that way. I fought with him for a year in court; finally my lawyer said to give him a divorce. I had opened a shop seven years before our divorce. The more I got into my work and became successful, the more withdrawn he became; he'd ignore the kids and me. I was struggling to save my marriage, so I went into therapy for myself, but he didn't want anything to do with that or with my gallery or me. It was my friends and family who helped me. He agreed to make a cabinet for the gallery, and then he sold the cabinet! It was just one kick after another.

When we divorced, I was in my late forties. I had to find a fulltime job—that slowed down my craftwork. Five years later I met my third husband. We were together for ten years, until his death. Again at that time, returning to my embroidery and weaving brought me home and bonded me with my ancestors. With that foundation, I could go on.

I try to give my children the same underpinning so they feel clear about themselves. My father told us girls things about the dances and songs and ceremonies. He said, "I'm going to tell you because I have mostly girls and if you marry outsiders—non-natives—and men that don't know our culture, you need to teach them. So I have to tell you." For that reason, too, we feel strong about who we are. We were taught to stand up for ourselves; even if someone pushes us down, we get up again.

Then he'd tell us the story of the Pueblo revolt in 1680, when many of the pueblos, including our family in the Tesuque Pueblo, rebelled against the Spanish colonization of New Mexico. Even then, our family felt strongly about defending what's right to keep our culture alive; we'd lose our lives for that principle if we had to.

Our ancestors are part of our spiritual being; I know they surround us throughout the day. We were taught they were a part of us in our daily lives; it's because they were so spirited and powerful that we're still here today. We believe in the same thing they believed in. When I think about my ancestors, I go back a thousand years. Today we have so much material stuff—technology, powerful machines, everything. Five hundred years ago when the Spanish came in, our people didn't have all those things that we have today, and yet they survived. That's why they inspire me.

My embroidery and weaving is spiritual practice: before I start working, I pray to my ancestors, because they did the work first. I say, "Come and help me" and ask them to show me how to put the thread and the design on the cloth. It's the same with everything I do: I pray before I weave or make pottery, so I feel connected with them.

What I know is what I learned from my ancestors, and they motivate me with their lives and their knowledge. When I sit down to work, I feel peaceful; it relaxes me and helps me feel calm and good about myself. I feel their presence so I know I'm getting their help.

On the walls, I have paintings of artwork from different artists; I especially like paintings of dancers. I'm living in the adobe house where I grew up. It has *vigas* (ceiling beams) and baskets hanging, making it a spiritual place for me. Sometimes I work in my room, or in the living room or kitchen.

I've been doing embroidery for a long time. I have all the designs in my mind, so I don't need to sit down with paper and pencil and figure out a design. I use the same patterns and designs my ancestors used and the traditional colors—green, black and red. I use the same design over and over, but I add my own touches to it; I may add a new line or pattern here or there on the kilt or sash.

With weaving and drum making and pottery, it's the same way. I always use the material that I think my ancestors used. The design and shapes have been handed down to me; I always use the traditional shapes of the pottery and at the end, I add some kind of a different pattern or shape from the traditional.

When I work, I want quiet. When I begin in the evening and the kids are in bed (I live with my daughter and her children), I feel at peace, especially if I'm working by myself and the phone's not ringing and the TV is off. I feel really good, and I'm into my inner self. Afterwards, I carry that feeling of peacefulness with me when I have to come back to reality, which is hard, but I do return to the world refreshed.

It makes me feel good that I'm home and doing what I really want to do. This is my work. It makes me feel comfortable and relaxed. More and more over the years, I've become calmer and less stressed. When the kids were younger, I couldn't get into my own work because I had to care for them; that's when I'd work late in the evening—that was my time.

This work is coming home to my true self—more so now than when I started doing embroidery when I was younger. I am pleased with the eight-to-five job I have now; I come home and do embroidery. After Christmas I started making a rain sash; that felt good. Now I want to keep going. I look forward to making pottery and drums. More and more, that is what I'll come home to.

Lee Roversi

Keeping the Organic Farm

Coming Home

When Lee Roversi was growing up in a picture-perfect family in an affluent neighborhood in suburban Connecticut, she had no idea that one day she'd end up with dirt under her fingernails as an organic farmer and innkeeper on the island of Kauai.

As the third of four children, Lee bought into her parents' comfortable lifestyle. She loved the peaceful, safe upper-middle class neighborhood where she grew up in the Fifties (they later moved to a similar neighborhood in the Boston suburbs). She would play Hide-and-Go-Seek and other games with the kids in her neighborhood until the sun went down and their parents meandered outside to fetch their children. She loved dressing up on Sundays and walking down the aisle of the Catholic Church with her hand in her father's and sitting quietly while the Latin hymns enveloped her.

Although her parents' marriage was a bit unorthodox at the time as her father was a second generation Italian from Queens and her mother, nine years younger, was a WASP from the Carolinas, they were very devoted to each other. They took a vacation together once a year and—also unusual in its day—they each took a separate vacation for a week: her father went on a Jesuit retreat and her mother played golf with her girlfriends. Her father was a midlevel executive and her mother, a strong southern woman, stayed home until all the children were in school and then got a job selling real estate.

Looking back on her childhood today, Lee realizes that the scene was just too good to be true. There must have been strains and struggles, the usual undercurrents that run in all families, but none of it was spoken or dealt with. Her mother, especially, must have felt the constraints of being a perfect New England housewife, though Lee doesn't recall them being played out, because that would have clashed with the Donna Reed image that her mother portrayed so well.

Even as a teenager, Lee didn't rebel. She remained the good preppy daughter. After two years of college and earning an Associate of Arts degree, she headed to the Big Apple to work in advertising. That was her first taste of life outside the bubble she grew up in. She prayed that a man would rescue her from the difficulties of making it on her own, and one did. She married a handsome ad man sixteen years her senior. Predictably, that marriage ended after two years.

Her divorce in her late twenties was the catalyst for Lee to begin looking at herself and figuring out what *she* wanted in life. She came to the realization that she was recreating the lifestyle that she grew up with—traditional, monetarily successful—but that was not who she was. She had never liked advertising and decided to quit her job. She began working out at a gym. Always happiest outdoors, she volunteered at the Audubon Society, which got her backpacking and into the wilderness, easing her soul. She spent a lot of her free time with an old friend and her baby helping to soothe her raw emotions after her divorce. At the same time, however, a craving for her own children, a feeling that had lain dormant, began to surface.

She met her second husband Chad, who became her partner and the father of her three children, in New York City. Initially, she found him handsome, sweet and sexy. As they moved into a more committed relationship, he was caring and steady, and he shared her love of the outdoors. He was a born enthusiast and would take on whatever was put in front of him, which led to their pattern of Lee taking charge and Chad following. Together they traveled, backpacked, and spent time at the beach. She felt that she could be herself with him.

Lee spent a few years freelancing while Chad pursued a career in acting and modeling. Although they had a diverse, interesting life in Manhattan, they knew it was temporary. Following their first son's birth, they bought a house in Old Greenwich, Connecticut, but after several years there, the town felt too homogeneous and limited for their tastes. In 1986, they sold the house to a huge profit, packed their three-year-old and newborn into their van, and traveled cross-country, visiting friends and national parks.

They ended up in Hawaii (her husband often went there to surf) and never looked back. They dreamed of a life without the constraints of working away from home, because they didn't want to leave their children to make a living. And they wanted to raise them in a community of like-minded people in contrast to what they considered the bland and somewhat conservative flavor of the east coast.

Within a few days of arriving, they bought a four-acre piece of land on the lush north shore of the island. It took them four years to build their house and a guesthouse that became a vacation rental. While they built a second eco-tourism cottage, they began growing and selling organic vegetables. No one else was doing that at the time so there was a huge demand for their crops. Their business kept getting bigger and bigger. Today North Country Farms grows and sells vegetables, fruit and flowers directly to fifty to sixty families each week and hosts intrepid travelers from around the world. The organic produce fills three acres. They also have orchard trees bearing avocados, limes, grapefruit, and mangos as well as a pineapple field, banana groves and tropical flowers.

Once they had achieved their dream, the question then became: What's next? Lee became more interested in answering soul-searching questions, such as, what am I about? Or, what makes my heart sing other than these three amazing children and this farm? Chad's personal pursuits revolved around his surfing and martial arts. Eventually their lack of communication became too huge a gap to bridge without desire, effort and therapy, which Chad was unwilling to participate in.

"I was a woman living in a dream, a dream that included a man to co-create it," Lee told me. "The dream was manifested bigger and better than we could have imagined but the relationship was sacrificed in the process. We grew older in completely different ways." There was never any screaming or shouting, but slowly and steadily, they grew apart and divorced in 2000.

Lee's first thought was to flee: sell the farm, get out of Kauai and start over. But once her emotions calmed down and she reviewed her options, she realized the farm was home in every sense of the word and it was not time for her or the children to leave. It was time for Chad to move on.

That was nine years ago. Today Lee's three children—Sky, twenty-seven; Nell, twenty-four; and Bay, twenty—live and work on the farm, but are pushing the limits of what Kauai offers. They each have left the farm for extended periods of time for travel, work and school as they try to figure out what to do with their own lives.

In the next section, Lee Roversi talks about what the decision to keep North Country Farms meant for her and her children, how she gained a new confidence and awareness of her abilities and talents at age sixty, and how keeping the farm has brought her home to a place of inner contentment.

In her own words....

I truly came home after my divorce from Chad. Reinvented as a single mom with a breathtaking farm to tend to, I had three home-businesses that anchored me here, and three simply amazing children who reminded me every day that I did the only thing possible by retaining our house and recreating a home.

My physical home is surely a place—this farm. But, my homecoming also means becoming comfortable in being myself and in being able to handle everything here on this farm.

We landed on this island twenty-two years ago, after moving here to follow a dream of a simpler, more wholesome life for us. We bought our property within three days. Neither of us is impetuous; it was truly meant to be. We didn't consciously decide to become farmers or anything, actually, other than residents of this amazingly beautiful north shore of Kauai! We planned on having enough money invested from the sale of our Connecticut house to coast a while, but the building of our home cost more than we anticipated.

So, along the way we planted a garden for ourselves and some fruit trees. I had done gardening and was always an outdoor gal. Then we saw that there was a screaming need for organic produce on the island. The rest just evolved, as did the eco-tourism aspect of the business, which is what really keeps me alive financially. We got into some debt, then we had a third child. But they were pretty sweet years when I look back.

The kids went to a wonderful small Waldorf school here. Chad and the other dads built the building. It was a beautiful experience. They were home-schooled after sixth grade, because the public school system here is abysmal and the private high school was too expensive and far away. I really liked having our kids home. Our farm is a rich experience — lots of life and business happening all the time, so there is not that isolation factor. My kids related daily to people of all ages and backgrounds, in addition to having a wonderful circle of friends. They were able to travel, both individually and as a family, without the constraints of school schedules.

The home schooling is part and parcel of the basis of our relationship. Educationally, there are holes in it, for sure. But my children are life-long learners and are grateful for not having had a traditional education. My experience was so different from theirs. I went to an excellent public grammar school and a really fine private high school. I never imagined that I'd chart a different course for them, but I did what I needed to do at the time.

We've had our challenges, but we stayed delightfully close through it all. Fortunately, my children have missed that difficult junior high experience when their tribe becomes their peers. For my children, their tribe was me and their auntie and cousins. Even today, they don't only look to peers for personal affirmation. That made a big difference.

Looking back on my relationship with Chad, I've been the mover and shaker from the get-go. I'm the one who said, "Let's sell the house" and "Let's move to Hawaii" and "Let's look into home birth." Chad's an amazing malleable human being, and he went along with a lot of my ideas. We worked well together.

We had this ideal of what we were going to do once we got here, and there was a lot of work and a lot of joy in manifesting it. Once the building was built, then we got the businesses going. All that got done in concrete, beautiful reality. Then, it was: the children are older, business is booming, the farm set up. So for me, the work then became: what am I about? I'm getting closer to fifty. What do I want for me? It became clearer to me and less clear to him. He was a little lost. I was more interested in meaningful physical encounters; he was still about quantity, not quality. I became more devoted to my yoga practice and put more energy into the children. He wanted to surf and do martial arts when he wasn't farming.

As we grew in different ways, our relationship grew more strained. There was not even a blowup. It was just a calm, constant distancing. Less and less talk. The flat-lining of a long-term marriage.

When our dream—of relocating to Kauai, building a home, a farm and a rural, more sustainable life—unraveled, I was afraid: afraid of the future and timid of making it on my own. My first thought was flight—get away from this community who viewed our scenario as perfect, our life and work together as idyllic—get away from the memories, the hand-built home, the gardens, the land where the dream was built and then shattered—get away from *him*. It was really difficult for me. I felt like I was a failure, that I was being judged by everyone on the island.

But, as I clarified my emotions and thoughts over time and sorted through all the choices, I realized that this *was* home. The single most defining decision was to keep the farm that my children and I were attached to. I realized that this strong and solid sense of place was going to help anchor us through the storm and would be vital to our moving forward with our lives.

I realized I needed to re-create home here for my children and me. I didn't need to go anywhere. It was so crystal clear. I thought it would be impossible to be happy again. Another thing seemed unfair: at a time when I was trying to make sense of things emotionally, there was so much practically that had to be figured out. I feel grateful that I had the internal guidance to sit tight enough to make that even more crystal clear.

Chad was not happy that I was keeping the farm, so we entered into mediation. It forced both of us to look at everything and hash it out. He wanted the farm sold, so he could get his money. He ended up staying on the island, but it took a long time for him to come around. I didn't know how I'd manage financially. It was a leap of faith, but it worked out more than nicely.

The subsequent hard work of figuring out how to do that, financially and actually, is now only a blur, although at the time, it involved massive sleep and weight loss as I navigated waters that were terrifying. (I sleep like a baby now. And I gained all the pounds back—also great. I love being sixty and wearing that estrogen-induced five extra pounds!) As I took on the responsibilities of continuing to create the dream solo, I gained such confidence and awareness of all my abilities and talents. I realized that I was the fuel that fired our family furnace all along!

I had lived all my adult life with a man—always looking for my reflection in that context—always trying to please, just as I had wanted to please my dad. Finding myself "alone" at fifty was a mammoth adjustment and not totally unpleasant! I could focus on my interests, my friends, my children—without the "distraction" of a partner. I got over the fear fairly fast and learned that I did not need a man to complete me. My husband's leaving did not diminish me.

I always thought I was capable, but like many of us, I leaned on my partner. In practical matters, he was strong to lean on. He built this house. But I've never leaned on him emotionally. I have a great circle of women friends. I see my life as a tapestry of dear ones that I have carefully woven and nourished. I treasure my relationships and take time to care for them. The women here on Kauai are a motley group. We have all come to this beautiful island with our stories, our history. But, mostly everyone's birth families are far away, so there is a need and a conscious thrust to create family here.

These women came and cared for me, buoyed me up, painted my toenails, poured me champagne, took me out to dinner, walked miles on the beach with me. They reminded me that I was beautiful, worthy and strong. And we continue to support and care for each other—celebrate together—cry together—and laugh lots.

To know that I could get to the other side of this emotionally was a very empowering thing. For years I felt like I had this weight on my shoulders and chest. I felt like I was dragging another human being along—spiritually and emotionally.

When I finally shed that weight, I felt liberated. I stepped up and reclaimed the capabilities and self esteem that my family had instilled in me at a young age. I don't know whether I lost it, but I had become more of a shadow of myself than I liked. And then Chad was constantly telling me that I had put the children first in our relationship. I'm not sure that was how it was, but that's how it felt to him. There was a freedom now in my being able to do just that. I was really there for them, not at my own expense, but quite at my pleasure.

My children are my deepest connection in this world. With them I am truly home. Simple. Clear. Being a mother has been my strongest spiritual growth. It is a passion for me. Striving to do this important "job" in a conscious way has brought me more joy than I can possibly express. Becoming a single mom when they all were either teens or on the cusp of becoming so, found us growing together at a very tender and sometimes tumultuous time.

They are all ready to break out from Kauai and have been for some time. The past six years they have each been away from the farm for lengthy stretches of time to study, work, or travel. I love having them here if they are content, but if their paths take them away, so be it. I'm sorry that our culture has gotten so far away from the concept of families living close to each other and interweaving their lives. That works for me, but only if my children would be content living here. I simply want them to be fulfilled and happy.

Even when they're not living here, we are constantly in touch. With my kids, it is pretty much all out there—the good, the bad and the ugly! We've communicated in a compassionate and clear fashion, consistently, since they were small. I've given that much focus, I suppose to avoid the path I experienced growing up.

Consequently, I felt empowered as a mom and quite capable and free as a businesswoman to reshape the businesses, as I wanted to. I could create the website that *I* wanted. I felt delightfully in charge of myself. And it felt real good. Of course, there were moments that were overwhelming but the pervasive strong, poignant feeling was one of strength and liberation.

Ironically, as I took on more responsibility after the divorce, I found I had more time for myself and relished that alone time. I had great freedom with my time and how I wanted to spend it, so I could get more into everything I loved. Time to read. Time to take beach walks. Oodles of time to give my children, time that we all treasured and needed. Time to write.

My journaling was a huge help in sorting out my emotions. I still write a lot but I don't sit down with my journals every day. I write a newsletter that I slip in with my veggies each week. Last week I wrote about being able to do a handstand in yoga and what that meant to me. It made me think. Writing is so affirming for me. It's a way of sharing what I think is worth sharing. There's something once again about being able to pass on our life-long wisdom. It's a marvelous feeling. When I get frustrated with my twenty-year-old son, I have to remember: why would I expect all my years of learning to be superimposed on him?

I have time now to deepen my yoga practice. When I was younger, my practice was more physical. Now I delved deeper, taking time to be expansive enough to see that there's something bigger than me. I've discovered my breath and use it to save me during anxious moments.

I loved the ceremony and the solace and the quiet I got from Catholicism growing up. I felt a connection to something larger, something cozy. As I grew up, I began doubting the tenets of my religion, but never really wanted to lose that thread that held me to a bigger presence. For a time, I rediscovered a similar sense in nature—backpacking and camping on weekends and vacations while I lived and worked in New York City. I reclaimed that same sense with my yoga practice.

Then, a wonderful sense of reverence and belonging came to me when my little children were enrolled in a Waldorf school here. In that school community I found a great respect for spirit—in the way the children were treated, in the way the community gathered for festivals (mostly Christian, but with clear pagan roots). There was consistently an awareness and respect for something beyond us and often connected with nature. It brought me "back home." And that strong spiritual pull is with me now: in my gardens, at the beach, in my yoga practice. It does not have a name or specific path—it just is, inside me, reflected in an ever-present sense of gratitude.

I feel really comfortable with myself now. That's a huge coming home. I'm sure I felt this way at different times before. I know I did when I was nursing my babies. There were a few other times I can say when everything coalesced into something perfect, but they didn't always last. This homecoming has lasted.

There was a very clear and special intention in founding this farm and the businesses on it. It is my passion to continue that. The children and I have a strong and solid sense of place being here. It was important to have that so that we can continue to grow and flourish, especially in the shadow of divorce. I continue to nourish a relationship with Chad so that our children can experience that warmth, but the divorce remains an emotional defining point for us all.

Before I came home to my true self, I was a woman who needed a man to co-create my dream. Our dream manifested itself bigger and better than we could have ever imagined, but we sacrificed our relationship in the process.

I am still a woman living a dream. Now, it is a solo dream. This farm is the place that is deeply and irrevocably home. As a woman, I am happier and more content than I have ever been before.

Paddy S. Welles

Love Conquers All

Hundreds of books have been written about love. Songs have been composed regaling its virtues. Romantic comedies find humor in the most unlikely matches and in the silliest maneuvers. But living in real life with a loved one is a whole other story. All our issues cannot be tied up in a neat little package at the end of the day. Nor can we ever know how we'll wind up relationship-wise in our sixties or seventies.

Paddy S. Welles, Ph.D., a marriage and family therapist, believes that our parents are our first love-teachers and, over the years, has learned her most enduring love-lessons from her father, a beloved minister. From a young age, she discovered that she could go to him with her questions and receive insightful answers. Years later, when he had retreated behind the veil of Alzheimer's, and she was going through a difficult time with her second husband, she asked him: "What makes all this pain worth bearing? What is important in all this insanity?" For a brief few seconds, his deep blue eyes looked directly at her and he replied, "Nothing but love really matters, honey. Nothing else. Only love."

That was her last question and his final answer. He died shortly after that. His words have stayed with Paddy for years and have helped her navigate through the rocky waters of her intimate relationships.

Growing up in North Carolina as the daughter of a minister and a "saint," as people called her mother, Paddy was taught to be "a good girl"—striving to be polite, friendly and respectful. She idolized her parents and wanted nothing more than to make them proud of her. But this became a heavy burden as she grew older and was haunted by her reputation as a "Goody Two Shoes."

She enjoyed school from the first moment of first grade, but was upset a few weeks into that year, when her father told her that God had called him to a different church, and they had to move from the small town of Sanford to Elizabeth City, near the Outer Banks. She will never forget the first time she saw the ocean. She and her little brother walked over the dunes holding their father's hands. "I thought my heart would burst," she recalls. "The vastness, the roar of the waves, the pelicans, seagulls, the sand between my toes...I still miss it with a physical ache when I'm away from it for too long."

Her family moved again when she was twelve, this time to Greensboro. In high school, her life revolved around school activities, her swim team, church and maintaining top grades. She never drank, smoked or cursed and was known as a high achiever, but also as naïve—believing a girl could get pregnant by sitting on a boy's lap.

She received a scholarship to a Baptist junior college, and two years later, transferred to the University of North Carolina in Chapel Hill. There, her world opened up. The majority of students smoked, drank beer and had sex. She realized they were still good, moral people. After developing friendships with many students from other countries and other religions, she realized that Christians alone did not hold "the keys to the kingdom," as she had once believed.

She married at twenty-two, still a virgin; and over the next six years, gave birth to four children. A few days after the birth of her third child, she realized that her marriage would not last 'til death do us part. This awareness seeped into her tired brain on a rainy Sunday after she returned from the emergency room with her two-year-old son, who had suffered third-degree burns after he fell into the vaporizer in flannel pajamas. Her three-year-old son had toys strewn all over the house and the newborn was whimpering. Her husband walked though the room, stepping over toys, and calmly announced that he was going fishing. She was speechless: Couldn't he see she needed help?

After her fourth child was born, Paddy enrolled in a child psychology course at a local university to try to understand one son's learning difficulties. By the time her youngest began nursery school, she had completed enough child psychology courses to be able to work at her daughter's nursery school. This allowed her to make a bit of money, which made her re-consider the idea of separating from her first husband.

She decided to move to Atlanta, where there was a good school for her son, and continued graduate school at Georgia State University. There she had her first beer and even tried to smoke pot. This was the Sixties after all.

After finishing a graduate degree in psychology and securing a job counseling female engineering students at Georgia Tech, she met her second husband, Tim, an engineer. A year later, she married him, acquired two stepsons, and moved to upstate New York to accept her first full-time employment as a college instructor. After their second year of marriage, they moved to France for almost five years. While in France, Tim had an affair, which shattered Paddy's belief in love—temporarily. After months of tumult, tears, therapy and tough choices, she was able to "almost" forgive him and continue the marriage—as a "work in progress."

Upon returning to Horseheads, New York, Tim became consumed with a passion for soaring gliders (planes without motors). For over twenty years, their only trips were to glider contests. During this period, Paddy learned that she could not compete with his affair with "fiberglass," and became involved with a man she admired who lavished attention on her. Her affair could have been motivated by "pay-back" time or her need to feel loved, which she had become an expert at denying.

After the children were in college, Paddy completed her Ph.D. and opened a marriage and family therapy practice. She continued to teach evening courses at the college, often putting twelve to fourteen hours a day into her work. Her husband, in response, had another affair. This time, she threw him out and was preparing to divorce him.

But instead, this became a powerful wake-up call to step back and re-evaluate her values and her life. Like the shoemaker whose children had no shoes, Tim felt lonely because Paddy gave so much of her time and energy to her clients' troubled marriages but had little left for her own. After intense soul searching, she realized how skewed her priorities had become and walked away from her successful therapy practice.

Paddy and Tim, who have been together thirty-five years, recommitted themselves to each other in a way that honored each of their needs and brought a new openness to their relationship. For Paddy, bringing a stronger sense of self to the relationship allowed her to be more honest about her personal needs for happiness. As we'll see in the next section, she gave herself permission *not* to sacrifice all of her needs to meet those of her husband.

At seventy-two, Paddy's life today revolves around writing books and the extended family. Besides her own four children, she has two stepchildren and eight grandchildren. Her books include *Are You Ready for Lasting Love? A Personal Guide to Creating Fulfilling Relationships* and *To Stand in Love: Untangling the Webs We Weave.* Although she has a Ph.D. in Child and Family Studies and was a college professor, she feels her greatest lessons have come from being a wife, mother, and grandmother. Her favorite place to think is close to water with a book and a journal. There she continues to seek to understand this complex thing we call love and to expand her definition of what home means to her.

In her own words....

I began to move away from my sheltered life, including my religious belief-system while a student at the University of North Carolina-Chapel Hill. Before then, I believed that I had a firm grip on "truth"—until a certain professor blew apart my illusion. I entered a Philosophy of Religion course feeling secure in my knowledge of the Bible and confident that I knew the theories of other major religions. I could discuss the basic ideologies of other religions as they related to my particular Christian beliefs, which I considered to be the ultimate truth. How embarrassing at *this* stage to admit that I was proud of my closed mind at that time. Because I had made superior grades on all the tests thus far, I expected that I'd ace the final and the course.

The professor barely passed me. After recovering from the initial shock, I went to see him, intending to correct *his* mistake. I'll never forget what he said to me: "I wanted to fail you because my primary objective in teaching this course was to open your mind to the possibilities of many truths. You came into this course with your little Christian belief system all tidied up. You never even took it out to examine it."

I literally began to shake from the impact of his words, as my faith in what I'd been taught to believe around religion and myself began to unravel. He challenged me to read Dostoevsky's *Brothers Karamazov* and write a paper analyzing how religion impacted each brother's life, and if I opened my mind, he would consider changing my grade. This experience was literally the "cracking of the cosmic egg" for me, for which I remain deeply grateful.

My divorce from the father of my children, becoming a single parent of four children and walking out of the organized church set the stage for having a delayed adolescence when I was in my late thirties. It required close to four chaotic years for those adolescent needs to be met before I became a more responsible adult with a committed interest in supporting learning-disabled children.

After I moved to upstate New York, I joined a college faculty, married my second husband with two young adolescent sons and tried to maintain an organized "happy home." There was little time for self-reflection. Two years later, we moved to Paris, where everything changed.

Tim had to leave several months before the children and I could finish what needed to be done at home. I felt like a whirling dervish. I believed that if I stopped whirling to even begin to consider how my life was going to change, I would never make it. I learned later that regardless of how prepared for changes we think we are, there are some things we cannot prepare for, since they are inconceivable until they happen.

My husband's affair with his French teacher was one of those things. It probably opened my mind to the complexities of human nature more than any other single event in my life up to that time. It definitely is one of the most significant markers of change on my life's path. It made me realize that sex, love and marriage can be totally independent variables—a new way of thinking for me. My French therapist helped me understand this at a much deeper level than I had previously. I began to realize that there are bigger problems than infidelity in marriage and when we allow sex to be the "biggie"—the reason to leave regardless of other good things, it could be a foolish decision (as it would have been for me at that time).

I began to understand the difference between forgiving and forgetting, the impossible part due to the emotional toll an affair takes on a marriage. Everyone going through such an experience has a choice to either eventually forgive or to remain miserable, filled with jealousy, anger and sadness. I had, by the time this happened, known many divorced couples who felt they had made tragic mistakes by leaving a marriage quickly without working through their issues, and therefore carried their same issues into their next relationship. I also had to carefully weigh the consequences of what a divorce would do to each of us and the children. Since I had resigned my position at the college, I had no job waiting, no place to go and was told that a divorce would adversely affect my husband's career. We would all end up in dire financial straights. Another huge factor was that Tim did not want me to leave—and worked hard to prove that.

I don't mean to suggest that I accepted what he had done without distancing myself—-saying some horrendously nasty things—and playing the "sinner-saint" role for a few weeks. But I didn't like myself in that role for long—realizing that during my lifetime, I had also committed a few sins.

I discovered aspects of myself that I would have denied prior to that time. I've never since been quite as judgmental, nor quite so sure of my own motives. The four years we spent in France stretched each of us far beyond what we would have imagined. Although I had not wanted to go in the beginning, I did not want to return to the U.S. after those years.

Following our return, life was filled with fairly normal events—children going to college, their marriages, my returning to graduate school to finish my Ph.D. And leaving my husband for another man. I separated from Tim, however, oddly enough, we remained friends throughout a two-year legal separation. During this time, the early Nineties, my eldest daughter lost a full-term baby. There had been no complications, no warnings. Nothing prior to this had even come close to touching the heartbreak of this event. I learned for the first time in my life that I had absolutely no way to help reduce my daughter's pain—that there comes a time when the only way through an event is to suffer with someone. Of everything that has ever happened to me, this alone made me come to grips with the depth of pain we humans are capable of bearing, and coming out the other side —deeply changed, but still breathing.

After this, I wanted nothing more than to create a safe space to heal. Since my husband is not the father of this daughter, he was not nearly so involved in this experience as I was, but he did want me to move back home, and I did. It was a good thing.

I returned to graduate school at Syracuse University, completed my Ph.D., opened my private practice and thought my life was finally settling down with less stress and upheaval. For the first time in my adult life, I felt content. I was professionally more successful than I'd ever dreamed possible. I loved my thriving therapy practice. In fact, I loved it to the extent that I often spent over twelve hours a day there, including weekends. I was also leading workshops and teaching courses on therapy. I felt as if I were really helping people.

The people I no longer took time to support were the ones I loved most: my husband, our grown children and grandchildren, and my friends. To show their respect for my time, my friends stopped calling. My children began every conversation with "Mom, I know you're busy, but..." I simply didn't get it, though there were plenty of warnings.

Tim and I did a weekend couples retreat to rekindle our love. It was wonderful. We returned home feeling very much in love, but as soon as we walked in the door, we resumed our "normal routine:" a quick breakfast together and then rushing our separate ways to do our important work. We were headed for a disaster.

And then "it" happened again: someone else showered the kind of attention on my husband that I had not given him in several years—except for the weekend retreat. While I was away in another country helping my daughter with her two young children while she had a third, Tim became involved with a younger woman who offered to crew (and screw!) for him during a glider contest. I didn't know what was going on, until I returned a day ahead of schedule. Oddly, this time there was only a dull ache—a blip in the road, so to speak, but I was done —I thought. I'd learned that I could be independent, that what we call love can be pretty fickle and that we all continue to seek it wherever we think we can enjoy it—especially if sex is involved. I threw him out immediately and filed for a divorce.

The day I was ready to sign divorce papers, he called and begged me not to do it. I hung up on him, but fell apart driving to the attorney's office. Praises be for an attorney wise enough to say he never allowed anyone to sign divorce papers when they were as upset as I was. He instructed me to call my husband and invite him to meet me for lunch. It was one of the most difficult calls I've ever made. It forced me to let go of my self-righteousness and pride. My husband canceled an important meeting to have lunch with me—-allowing me to feel important to him for the first time in several years.

I became aware that I had spent a great deal of my life trying to feel important to large groups, because it was easier than trusting any one person whom I loved to deem me important. I could hide my negative traits from groups, but the person with whom I had lived for over twenty years knew them well.

After remaining separated for several months, we made a re-commitment, but with a different set of expectations. I walked away from my fulfilling therapy practice and began to redefine love from a deeper perspective, one that involves increased attention, time, and energy. He slowed down a bit and committed himself to expressing more honest feelings rather than repressing them. This does not mean that every day has been easy, but now we deal with everything in a more honest and supportive way.

We recognized our differences and realized we needed to allow each other the space to live them out. He wanted to spend most of his time in the air (flying gliders and planes) while I much preferred being in and close to water. Compromise, rather than feeling I had to sacrifice the things I loved to be assured of his love, was a new way of interacting for me. I did agree to take a few flying lessons so I could land a plane or glider, if something happened to him while I was in the same flying object. Much to my surprise (and his), I discovered that I enjoyed flying and my instructors reported that I would become a good pilot. I became a licensed glider and power pilot—one of the oldest (at fifty-four) females to be licensed in the U.S.

For over twenty-two years, our only travel experiences had been to glider contests, with my "crewing" for him—washing bugs off glider wings, driving hundreds of extra miles with the glider trailer to rescue him when he "landed-out"— often to places I would not have driven—even in my worst nightmares! However, ten years ago a friend invited me to go to Bhutan with a group of people interested in different cultures and lifestyles. This was a critical choice for me. I knew I wanted to go. I wanted to break away from the routine of only traveling to glider meets, but I felt guilty approaching the subject. Rather than ask, I told Tim I was planning to go. He was not happy, to say the least, but something in me had shifted and he realized it. This trip established a new kind of independence for me, and one I will not willingly give up.

Since then, I have made many trips alone or with friends. Alaska and Antarctica were two that proved to be major wake-up events—to the awareness of what is happening to our planet, as well as developing friendships that have influenced my life. My confidence and independence have been strengthened considerably through these travels. However, another important shift has also occurred: I can say "no" without guilt—well, without too much guilt.

It has become very clear to me that I need alone time as much as together time. Not only is it necessary for writing, but necessary for me to take a break from trying so hard to please everyone else in my life. This quality of feeling responsible for pleasing everyone whom I love (even sicker, I've even spent many years trying to please people I didn't even like) is slowly disappearing. I've finally accepted that I do not need everyone's admiration, and I do not need to please everyone—impossible anyway! I've given up hypocrisy in the last few years, and it is so freeing—yes, so coming home to my real self.

Five years ago, I purchased a small cottage on a lake in Canada. The minute I arrive at the top of the drive to the cottage, I feel at home. Ironically, my great-grandparents were from the same area, but I didn't know that when I purchased the property. I love being close to water, having a chance to be alone or with a few precious friends I've made there. Several have become almost a blended family of choice.

My family of origin had great expectations of me. Both of my parents were high achievers, outstanding and talented people. As their first-born, I assumed I had to be the same way. I did everything I possibly could to live up to them, so they would be proud of me. For over fifty years, I equated this with love. The people I now love unconditionally have helped me drop that variable from my love equation and allowed me to accept myself without trying so damn hard to be more and more and more. I was worn out by feeling obligated to do everything anyone asked of me. I have finally learned to say no.

My journey home to myself has come to mean that I've finally learned that I don't have to be "the best" to be loved and that the only thing that really matters is to be open to unconditional loving relationships. This requires developing the understanding that love will involve pain, compromise, and a need to forgive (myself, as well as others). It means that I am willing to accept myself without denying my faults and that I will not blame others for things that cause problems in my relationships. It does not mean that I have to sacrifice myself to obtain love. It means I understand that I am free to say no, and will give others the same freedom. It means giving up trying to control another's behavior or feelings.

Because I am a passionate person, I will continue to feel all emotions—I'll always be angered by injustice, I'll never love everyone, but I'm developing more compassion toward most—even those I don't particularly like. I'm much more comfortable in my own skin than I've ever been.

Home is where my heart lives, either with someone I love or with someone whom I share a sense of belonging and total acceptance of each other. Home allows me the freedom to be who I am, sitting on a sand dune, standing on a mountaintop, or hiking through deep woods after a new snow. Home can be a canoe, a tent, a cabin or even a book. Home is that place where I can laugh or cry without explanation because people who love me understand. They are a part of home too.

Victoria Zackheim

Becoming a Somebody

Victoria Zackheim, a writer, editor and creative writing instructor, grew up wanting to be a somebody. But not just anybody. She wanted to be somebody famous, somebody whose singing voice would bring a crowd to its feet... somebody who would make her parents proud.

Raised in Compton, in South Central Los Angeles, during the 1950s, Victoria was part of one of the few Jewish families in a town divided by a railroad track. The whites lived on one side and the African-Americans, on the other. Victoria's family lived on the white side, but her father, a pro-integration liberal, was principal of the all-African-American high school. From the time she was in kindergarten, she was made to suffer for her father's politics and his successes. His sports teams were better than the white high schools', he had more students going on to higher education, and he hired the "problem" teachers—the Jews, the blacks and the gays—and he gave them the freedom to be the exemplary teachers they already were.

All this infuriated people, and they vented their anger on Victoria and her sister. Her sister was more reticent so did not suffer as much. Victoria would speak out for her beliefs, but underneath, was so insecure that any student or teacher's teasing (the teachers were a part of it too) could easily reduce her to tears. It was not uncommon for her to run home crying because she was called a "nigger lover."

There were few places where Victoria felt safe. She did not even feel secure in her own home, because people threw firecrackers at their house. On one occasion, a car drove by and a bullet was shot through their front window. Consequently, she grew up feeling lonely, isolated and afraid for her physical safety. When she did seek refuge, it was often in the home of friends in the black community.

Her father had a lot of expectations for his daughter. While he was very encouraging and told her she could be anything she wanted, there was a catch in this praise: she had the responsibility to fulfill *his* hopes and dreams. In reality, he spent more time with his students than with his own children. "Had I received the attention he gave to his students, I wouldn't have been so insecure," Victoria told me. Her mother had a chronic illness and struggled to be part of her daughters' lives.

It was freeing to go off to college where no one knew who she was, but she had no idea how to be. She lacked confidence and was a mediocre student. She got married at twenty, the summer before her senior year, to a sweet, innocent boy of her age.

Her husband was more interested in business than politics, so she felt she had to stifle her political passions. Not knowing who she was, she tried to fit into his family's well-organized structure. They were quite conservative, and she felt that she could not measure up to their expectations about how to dress and how to act. In retrospect, she believes that had she been more mature, she might have understood how to make the marriage work. Despite her liberal bent of standing up for the underdog, she had never learned how to stand up for herself. His family wanted a wife who was more traditional, but this little voice in her head kept asking: What about me?

Victoria got a master's in speech pathology so she could work with deaf students, but that wasn't what she really wanted to do. She had wanted to be a doctor when she entered university, but feared that, at age seventeen, she was ill-prepared for the demanding courses in chemistry, physics, German, and philosophy required in the first semester, and she abandoned that path. She worked briefly as a speech therapist with post-stroke patients but quit when her son and daughter were born. Victoria and her husband divorced in the early Eighties after fifteen years of marriage. She worked for an ad agency for a number of years and then started freelancing. When her children were at university, she went to France and remained for five years, living a life she had long dreamed of. In 2001, she self-published her first novel, *The Bone Weaver*, and sold three thousand copies out of the trunk of her car.

In recent years, she has edited three anthologies: *For Keeps: Women Tell the Truth About Their Bodies, Growing Older, and Acceptance; The Other Woman: Twenty-one Wives, Lovers, and Others Talk Openly About Sex, Deception, Love, and Betrayal*; and most recently, *The Face in the Mirror: Writers Reflect on Their Dreams of Youth and the Reality of Age*. Her fourth anthology, *He Said What?!* will be published in February 2011.

Two years ago, Victoria would have told you that life was good: She loved the challenge of developing the anthologies and working with the authors throughout the editing process. Promoting the books to rave reviews gave her some of the recognition she yearned for. Her granddaughters, now seven-year-old twins who live twenty minutes away from her in San Francisco, brought her great joy. But then, everything changed. In the summer of 2008, she fell down the stairs in her loft. That fall dramatically altered her life. Actually, her life *outwardly* did not change that much: she still describes her life as good and fulfilling. The internal shifts, however, were transformational.

As she relates in the next section, Victoria Zackheim discovered her fragility, came to terms with her mortality, and developed a newfound ability to accept help from friends and family. But most importantly, she finally understood the true meaning of being a somebody, and the wisdom she learned has brought her home to her deepest self at sixty-four years of age.

In her own words....

When we're growing up, our parents want us to succeed: to have that *sense* of success, plus it makes them feel validated. I grew up with a very powerful need to be a somebody. That meant the opposite of being a nobody. I worked hard to make my mark in speech pathology and as a freelance writer. I wanted to be acknowledged.

After my divorce, I had to make a living so I joined an ad agency. I loved writing ad copy, even if I didn't believe in what I was selling. When I became a freelance writer, I had the opportunity to write for a variety of clients. I joined a team of political writers whose goal was to elect Democratic candidates—right up my alley! My most memorable was writing stump speeches for Alan Cranston, at that time the senior member of the U.S. Senate. The senator and I were introduced to each other several times but, perhaps ironically, he never remembered me!

When my children went off to college, I decided to go to Paris for a few months to figure out what to do next. I ended up staying five years. Living alone, away from family and friends, I began to confront myself. I wondered: How could I have been so naïve as to believe that finding a profession I loved meant I had found myself? Those years, in which I learned to live completely alone and rely only on myself, proved to be the greatest learning experience of my life. I learned that I could count on myself, that I had the wherewithal to live a full and exciting life, and that I was as adaptable as I had suspected, but had never really been tested. In a sense, I met myself for the first time, and I liked that woman.

I seriously considered permanent residency in France, but I had young adult children in California and knew they would marry and start families, and there was no choice...I could never miss being part of that. Also, my mother was aging, and I felt the need to be closer and give her my support. In addition, I had finished my novel and sensed that I needed to be in the states if I expected to publish it.

Once I returned from Paris, reality set in. I bought a home. I was back in the mortgage-paying, having-to-earn-a-living mode. Also, the lifestyle I had enjoyed in Paris was impossible for me here. Geographically speaking, it's thrilling (and convenient) to have all of your dear friends within thirty minutes by Metro. There was a spontaneity to life in Paris that doesn't...and probably can't...exist in the Bay area.

Nonetheless, life was basically good. I edited several anthologies and sold them to good publishing houses. I was constantly on the run with interviews and book signings. I was not so much driven as motivated. I had this opportunity in my sixties and I wanted to maximize that. I love to be with my two granddaughters and *prefer* to be with them, but I have to work. I was, and still am, very involved with a documentary film company in New York City. There was always a lot going on, which is still the case. But there wasn't much introspection because I didn't take time to do that. I was in the flow.

In August 2008, ten days before my son's wedding, I was supposed to fly to New York to be interviewed on Good Morning America radio and cable to promote the paperback launch of my anthology, *The Other Woman*. I was carrying an outfit down the carpeted stairs of my loft to run out to meet a friend who was going to help me find a scarf to go with it. I felt the fabric wind around my ankle, and I remember thinking, oh shit. Next thing I remember, I was on the ground and couldn't lift my head off the floor. My head was pounding. Fortunately, I could reach my cell phone and called my daughter. I was also able to pull open the door and wedge my foot in the door so she could get in.

Next thing I remember is my daughter, my granddaughters and my neighbor being there. I could hear my daughter telling her girls, "Just sit on the steps, Mima will be fine." There were firemen, an ambulance, a trip to the head trauma center. "Open your eyes," they kept telling me, but I was thinking, "It's so quiet in here. Do I have to open my eyes?" I knew I had hit my head. I heard talk of a broken skull, a broken arm, broken ribs. As it turned out, I had not fractured my skull, or broken my arm or any ribs. But I did have one nasty concussion.

I cancelled the trip to New York and ended up with a terrible problem with memory, a cherry red eye and lots of swelling on my face. The red eye disappeared (thanks to some good makeup), but I couldn't remember the names of people at my son's wedding. I still have a few memory problems a year later. I don't remember the impact of actually hitting my head. My balance was off for a long time. Maybe two months ago, it came back again. I'm probably 99% recovered physically. I'm doing very well.

One thing that really surprised me was the people who stepped forward. When you go through a difficult time, you can see who's there for you. The first friend who arrived to take me to the market was a psychotherapist and author who works a forty to sixty-hour week. Many friends and family kept in contact, checking on me daily. It was very touching. And then, I had to learn to accept their help. The whole process was an affirmation of my friendships.

My emotional and spiritual recovery is another story. I'm more cautious physically about how I move. More than that, I've slowed down a bit; I've given myself time to reflect. It's not just "Stop and smell the roses." I've removed the importance of things that I gave too much importance to. I get very intense about having to do *everything* when I'm on a book tour, for example. Then I stop. Control has always been a big issue for me. I'm learning to give up some of that control. I'm more trusting of other people to do what they've been hired to do, or what they've offered to do. I'm less arrogant and more willing to admit that I can't do it all. A part of me still warns that if I don't keep pushing and doing, things won't get done, but I'm beginning to be easier on myself—and maybe on other people as well.

I always expect others to have the same level of intensity as I do. I burn myself out — physically and emotionally—with every book. I have to ease up, back off a bit and let the universe do what it's going to do. There are alternatives. I could hire a publicist, but I do myself what I'd hire someone to do.

What I've discovered is that some people find my comfort with myself difficult to deal with because they're still doubting, still pushing to prove themselves. When I sell a book, I can feel their response: "Now you can go to the next step." What does that mean? For me, it's not about the next step any more. It's about doing what I do and enjoying that. And if I sell a book, that's a nice by-product, but it doesn't change how I feel about myself. It's not part of my definition of who I am. It doesn't change *me*.

This attitude has taken 95% of the pressure off me to succeed. If you had asked me five years ago, I would have said that if I don't have the need to succeed, there must be something wrong with me. Now, I'm just doing what I do and things are working out just fine. I teach in the UCLA Extension Writer's Program, and I love it. The classes I teach for them are online and the students live all over the world. It's wonderful, challenging work. As for the message *You've got to succeed. You have to prove to everyone you're capable so they'll ask you back*, I don't worry about this anymore. I'm doing what I love to do. If there's a benefit, that's wonderful. If not, I can take that skill and apply it to something else. That's where the biggest changes have come.

But even politically, I've changed. I'm not more conservative, but I'm more accepting of people who don't agree with me. Now, I don't cut off a friendship because someone is a Republican. My college roommate supported Bush. How can you love someone who loves George Bush? Well, guess what? You can. The edges become softer, less defined. The sharp corners become more rounded. I remember dating a man, and he said to me, "I can't believe you're the same Vicki Z. You're so unlike your reputation. Some people thought you were a bitch." What I discovered was that, as a young woman, I had sharp corners that kept people at a safe distance. I was, and still am, intensely private.

People didn't realize that I was protecting myself. I *did* soften over the years. Since I fell, I realize that I'm more willing to acknowledge my feelings. Because of my accident, I'm willing to admit that I have all the same human frailties as everyone else. And that doesn't weaken me; it makes me stronger. In another way, it makes me more protective of myself: I was so caring about everyone else in the past. This is the first time I've ever been truly concerned with my own physical well being and paid attention to myself. I'm more vulnerable and at the same time, I'm the center of my own universe and that's okay. That's new for me.

Editing the anthologies has helped me share more of my feelings in writing as well. When authors send me their essays, where they dig into parts of their lives that they have never touched before, it pushes me to be more honest and more present with my own writing. I used to write more superficially. I'm not doing that any more. In *The Other Woman*, I was able to write about being a divorced woman in a relationship with a divorced man. By that time, our relationship had ended, and I hadn't fallen yet, so I could write with some distance. But when I wrote an essay for my new book *The Face in the Mirror*, I was able to get deeper into the pain of childhood with more honesty.

I'm working on a novel, and I think a lot about the main character, who is too shallow and needs to be re-thought. She is not me. Not that I was shallow before, but I was only willing to share so much of me. My dear friends know what's under the protective surface. I've learned to trust them, and that trust has never been easy for me. I was brought up believing I shouldn't be trusting, yet trusting I was...alas. You know, the old heart on the sleeve. I've lost a lot of the reticence I once had. If you and I were out together and someone said something rude to you, I would have had no problem addressing it, but if they had said something rude to me, I would have smiled through my hurt and tried to deflect it.

Not any more. I'm much more confrontational for myself—not in an angry way. It's 'I have rights, I'm a respectable person.' If someone says something to me that's unkind, I'll say, "I don't know why you're using that tone of voice with me, I don't deserve it." It's very empowering and freeing. Wow, where did that come from? I've always been an advocate for others. Now I'm advocating for myself. That's different.

Growing up with an ill parent, the world is very frightening. I had never given myself credit for what I earned. Now I'm aware of what I'm achieving. Instead of being self-effacing, I'll say, "Thank you for acknowledging that. That's important to me." That self-effacement was a major part of my personality for a long time. I know that what I do with these anthologies is very good work. I *am* a good editor, probably more than I am a good writer. I could do only anthologies, but they're very time consuming and pay too little. If I were looking for a way to earn a living, it would not be through anthologies!

The accident has also changed my spirituality. I've never been very spiritual (though many of my friends are), and my parents were both red diaper babies. There's a difference in how I look at things now.

When I say, "God willing," I'm not saying it with a smile afterwards. I've always felt there was something bigger than us. Since my fall, despite the fact that everything in the world is spinning today, I actually have the greatest sense of inner peace.

I've never had a problem being alone. I enjoy my own company, I love to read and walk. I've never been bored, even as a child. What's changed for me is how I spend my alone time now. It's not being alone and thinking, *I've got this time, what am I going to work on?* It's simply enjoying this time. I'm alive; I'm going to turn sixty-five soon. I can't believe I've lived that long. Sometimes I feel like I'm thirty until I try to do something very physical...or look in the mirror!

Now, I can just sit quietly and be with myself and be completely at peace and not feel that I have to achieve something. I'm enjoying my own company and being alive. Between getting older and the experience of the fall, I'm able to reflect and be more in touch with these things. The fall was important for me because I wasn't that aware of getting older. I'm in my sixties, but I'm convinced I can still do things I could do in my thirties. Other than my novel, all of my books happened in my sixties. The most exciting, creative work I've ever done, including my documentary film work with On the Road Productions, has been in the last few years.

After I fell, it marked the first time I felt old. I was bruised physically and emotionally. For a time, I was even cautious about driving. I realized: This is what old age feels like. Most of that went away as I healed. But it left behind a very clear notion of what it means to be sixty-five. My father died at sixty-four, yet in some ways I'm just starting. I feel like I'm in the prime of my life. I'm a fairly energetic person. Do I wish I were younger? No, my life is much richer now. I have enough energy to sustain me in what I'm doing. At forty, I wouldn't take the time to be as introspective. I walk by a store today and see my reflection and think, who *is* that old woman? It's got to be me. I could dye my hair and have liposuction, but I don't choose to. I know a lot of women who aren't comfortable in their bodies, or with the woman they are, and I find this sad.

It's possible that all these changes might have taken place as I aged, but not with the same dramatic impact. Losing my balance, some hearing, memory...brought home how vulnerable I am, and how quickly everything can be lost. Certainly the aging process would have brought with it a new awareness of how precious life is, but this fall transformed that awareness from a little melody playing in the background of my mind to a *fortissimo* movement worthy of Beethoven.

I wasn't actively trying to change. Rather, it was a profound and dramatic awareness, like a window suddenly blowing open to a world of possibilities and a life yet to be lived. I've always had a deep appreciation for being alive...in my case, that comes from a childhood formed by my mother's serious illness. So I would not say the fall was a wake-up call to something I *didn't* have, but an intensifying of what I do have...and will continue to have...hopefully.

I have a very different perspective of my life now. For the first time, I realize I *can die.* I was very ill when the children were babies and recovered just fine. I haven't been in the hospital since 1972. I'm not on any medication, and I rarely think about when I'm going to die. It's very frightening, tumbling through the air and landing on your head. It changed my attitudes about how I live my life. It's not as if I went from being a dishonest person to an honest one; it's that the importance of things has shifted for me. I've always appreciated my family and my friends. My son and his wife are expecting twins in early May, and I'm so aware of my gratitude for being here to share their joy. So, it's not appreciation that has changed but the degree of appreciation.

It's best to describe it in color. Everything had color, but the colors are more intense now. It's like looking at the world through a richer film. It's not that I see a color differently. My whole world is colored differently. Things that had a richness before have a greater richness now. My grandchildren: I see them in a more nuanced way. I'm much more present and allow them to be more present. I'm more willing to share myself in a deeper way. I was always a good listener but now I'm more willing to share of myself. I feel that changing.

Before my accident, I was desiring to please and be accepted with little recognition of who I was, or why. Now I feel confident and prepared to take risks. I'm not worried about being judged, but only about exploring as many creative possibilities as I can before I'm too old to explore. I no longer need to look into the faces of friends, children or even strangers to determine who I am. I know.

After six decades, I finally understand that being a *somebody* is not the opposite of being a *nobody*. As I wrote in my essay for *The Face in the Mirror*, it has nothing to do with being famous, recognized or admired. Being a somebody simply means being who I am and living that way. Being a somebody is being myself.

Recommended Reading

This list includes books that were helpful to me in my research as well as books written by the women featured in this book.

Arrien, Angeles. *The Second Half of Life: Opening the Eight Gates of Wisdom*. Boulder, CO: Sounds True, 2005.

Blair, Pamela. *The Next Fifty Years: A Guide for Women at Midlife and Beyond.* Charlottesville, VA: Hampton Roads Publishing Co., 2005.

Borysenko, Joan, Ph.D. *A Woman's Book of Life: The Biology, Psychology, and Spirituality of the Feminine Life Cycle.* New York: Riverhead Books, 1996.

Feldt, Gloria. *Behind Every Choice is a Story*. Denton, TX: University of North Texas Press, 2003.

___________ *The War on Choice: The Right-Wing Attack on Women's Rights and How to Fight Back*. New York: Bantam Books, 2004.

___________ *No Excuses: 9 Ways Women Can Change How We Think about Power.* Berkeley, CA: Seal Press, 2010.

Green, Cinny. *Trail Writer's Guide.* Santa Fe, NM: Western Edge Press, 2010.

Heilbrun, Carolyn G. *The Last Gift of Time: Life Beyond Sixty*. New York: The Dial Press, 1997.

Pinkerton, Elaine. *From Calcutta with Love: The World War II Letters of Richard and Reva Beard*. Lubbock, TX: Texas Tech University Press, 2002.

_______________ *Beast of Bengal*. Clifton, VA : Pocol Press, 2005.

Porter, Kathleen. *Ageless Spine, Lasting Health: The Open Secret of Pain-free Living and Comfortable Aging.* Austin, TX: Synergy Books, 2006.

Ramsey, Valerie with Heather Hummel. *Gracefully: Looking and Being Your Best at Any Age.* New York: McGraw-Hill, 2008.

Rountree, Cathleen. *On Women Turning 60: Embracing the Age of Fulfillment.* New York: Three Rivers Press, 1997.

________________ *On Women Turing 70: Honoring the Voices of Wisdom.* San Francisco: Jossey-Bass Publishers, 1999.

Schachter-Shalomi, Zalman. *From Age-ing to Sage-ing.* New York: Warner Books, 1995.

Sheehy, Gail. *New Passages: Mapping Your Life Across Time.* New York: Random House, 1995.

Welles, Paddy S., Ph.D., *Are You Ready for Lasting Love: A Personal Guide to Creating Fulfilling Relationships.* New York: Marlowe & Co., 2001.

Zackheim, Victoria. *For Keeps: Women Tell the Truth About Their Bodies, Growing Older, and Acceptance.* Berkeley, CA: Seal Press, 2007.

____________ *The Other Woman: Twenty-one Wives, Lovers, and Others Talk Openly About Sex, Deception, Love, and Betrayal.* New York: Grand Central Publishing, 2008.

_____________*The Face in the Mirror: Writers Reflect on Their Dreams of Youth and the Reality of Age.* Amherst, NY: Prometheus Books, 2009.

LaVergne, TN USA
23 September 2010
198076LV00001B/102/P

9 781935 604020